God's Frozen People

God's Frozen People

A Book For and About Christian Laymen

by

Mark Gibbs and T. Ralph Morton

Philadelphia

THE WESTMINSTER PRESS

LIBRARY OF CONGRESS CATALOG CARD NO. 65-10952

Published by The Westminster Press
Philadelphia, Pennsylvania ®

PRINTED IN THE UNITED STATES OF AMERICA

Contents

In all our criticism and sometimes near despair of the institutional Church, it should never be forgotten that many powers and possibilities really exist in it, but often in captivity; they exist as frozen credits and dead capital.

Hendrik Kraemer, *A Theology of the Laity,* p. 176

There is a great deal of talk in church circles at the present time about the importance of the laity. But the question is approached almost invariably from the wrong end. What is usually meant is that more laymen should come in and give their support to the Church as it is. That is just what a large number of the best lay people at present standing on the fringe will not do.

J. H. Oldham, *Life Is Commitment,* p. 89

Introduction to the American Edition

Let us admit quite frankly what this book is and is not. In the first place, it is not a piece of original thinking, a major contribution to the doctrine of the church, or a historical treatise on clergy and laity. Almost everything we have written can be found in the major works on the clergy-laity theme. Veteran "ecumaniacs" who have been active in the World Council of Churches movement since it was founded, and who have been "rediscovering the laity" since 1945 — this book is not for you.

It is for God's ordinary people, for the men and women — and even more for those young men and women — who are to be found inside and outside our Sunday congregations, who are sincerely concerned with the Christian faith, who are nevertheless a little unhappy with the church around the corner, and who want something in fairly blunt language, which they can chew over, and argue about, and maybe pray a bit about. GOD'S FROZEN PEOPLE is intended as an experiment in informal teaching for ordinary Christians; that is why we asked the British and American publishers to get it out in paperback form from the start.

Secondly, this book is not an encyclopedia on the whole duty of the lay Christian. There's a lot left out. We do not say much about his devotional life, about his sex life, about his doubts as to whether God is "up there" or "down there," about the bomb or the Sacraments. We give fair warning that we may try to write something together on lay Christians and worship (to be called, obviously, "God's Lively People"); but for the present, we offer, rather, more comments about the temptations to keep up with the Joneses than about the dangers of keeping down with the Robinsons.

Thirdly, this American edition is not an attempt to tell our transatlantic cousins what is wrong with their churches! We have attempted to iron out some of the British jargon and to make our chapters more easily intelligible to American readers. But this is, frankly, a book that comes out of the British situation. Often enough it seems to us (from an admittedly slight acquaintance with American church life) that many Christians in the States share the same frustrations as any others, at least in Western Europe. There are also obvious differences: a cynic might say that the British layman stays away from the church which he vaguely respects, while the American layman dutifully attends on Sunday—with his mind more than half elsewhere. Certainly many of our shabby and ill-financed British churches compare dismally with the smart and even luxurious church plants to be found in most American suburbs—though not so often, perhaps, in the inner-city areas. It is entirely likely that denominational bureaucrats in Philadelphia or New York are more adequately remunerated than their counterparts in London or Edinburgh. Nevertheless, we are hopeful that the basic arguments of our book will arouse plenty of lively comment across the Atlantic; and we are encouraged in this by the most friendly reception which advanced copies of the British edition have received.

We have had fun writing this book. It is the result of a dialogue that has gone on between us for over eight years; for it was in 1955 that the senior member of the partnership asked the other to give a week's lectures on the island of Iona on the Ministry of the Laity. This was part of the summer season of lectures and discussions that are arranged each year, both for the newly joined permanent members of the Community and for visitors to the island. Each year since then we have both tried out different ideas and chapters of this book, not only with very many Iona discussion groups, on the island and on the mainland, but with a wide variety of other groups of both clergy and laity. Somehow or other we reduced our conclusions to print.

It is possible that some may feel that we have been a little overcritical of the churches as they are; and indeed there is at the moment a good deal of sharp criticism coming from radically-minded Christians in Britain, in Europe, and in North America. This is producing a certain mutter of "disloyalty" from more traditionally-minded church members. We are certainly not anxious to offend people; we have spoken bluntly only because silence inside the church on some of these matters is in fact a false loyalty — which offends those outside our church walls and makes them stumble. And if there has to be a choice between upsetting some of God's faithful veterans in the congregations or failing to serve some of God's frozen and lonely people on the fringe of our churches, then it seems to us clear which is the choice we must make, according to all that the New Testament teaches.

We are deeply grateful to all those who have helped us with the writing of this book, and with the discussions on Iona and elsewhere which have helped to shape its chapters. We cannot mention them all by name here; but we should like to express our particular thanks to Dr. J. W. Howie, who gave the manuscript such detailed criticism, and to Mrs. E. Black, Mrs. G. McIlwraith, Mrs. C. Morton, and Mrs. M. Platt for their invaluable secretarial assistance. We are most grateful for the helpful criticisms we have received from Dr. John Casteel and Rev. Scott Paradise in preparing this American edition.

We acknowledge very gratefully our debt to the writers and publishers whose works are quoted in our book, and thank SCM Press, Ltd., for permission to quote from J. H. Oldham's *Life Is Commitment,* Geoffrey Bles, Ltd., for J. B. Phillips' *Letters to Young Churches,* and The Seabury Press, Inc., for Hans-Ruedi Weber's *Salty Christians.*

M. G.
T. R. M.

1. *What Is a Layman?*

Ask a doctor what he means by the word "layman," and he will say, "Somebody who hasn't been trained to understand medicine." And that is one normal meaning of "layman" today — someone who is an amateur, who doesn't understand, who isn't an expert. In that sense of the word, this book wants to abolish the Christian "layman": we want to make Christian experts instead.

An Episcopalian clergyman of a hundred years ago, if asked what he meant by the word "layman," would probably have replied: "One of my flock. One of the congregation, one of the ordinary Christian people whom I have to instruct and lead." And a good many church people of all denominations would still agree in their hearts with this, although non-Episcopalians might not put it quite in this way. The assumption is that a layman is one of the privates in God's army; and the officers are the clergy. As if there were two grades of Christian — first class: parsons; and second class: laity. The first class have the job of running the church, of deciding the doctrine and administering the Sacraments and preaching the sermons and, above all, setting a good example. They have to be first-class in moral standards. The second-class Christians, the laity, don't have quite the same status in the church (or probably in heaven hereafter), *nor do they have the same responsibilities,* either for "the church" or for their moral standards. Such a distinction entirely suits many lay people, who can therefore be content with a much lower standard of life for themselves, while half laughing at and half admiring the "higher" standard which they see the parson struggling to maintain. Nor does it altogether displease many clergy, who find in the heroic role they are expected to play some psychological compensation for their diminished importance in national and local affairs. At least they can accept their calling to be lights in a dark world—and even their increasing isolation from men and women is, after all, one of the penalties of being God's chosen few.

There has been a certain development from this attitude in recent years. The dumb and faithful flock are now expected to do a little more for the church than in the past, largely because there has been (in Britain, at any rate) such a shortage of clergy. They are asked to help out in several ways. In the first place, they are expected to raise a good deal more money than in the past (by such campaigns as "planned giving"), and to contribute their time in looking after church accounts, church premises, and similarly "worldly" things, in order to free the minister for more "spiritual" matters such as preparing the Sunday sermons. More than this, they may even be expected to act as some kind of substitute clergy, as local preachers, lay readers, Sunday school teachers, even sick visitors or street corner evangelists — again, helping out the shortage of clergy by doing whatever minor duties (with careful supervision) can be delegated. Of course, all this is a rather unfortunate use of "unqualified" or substitute man or woman power — it is always much more satisfactory if you can have a clergyman (even an assistant minister) for your services. And it certainly does not upset the traditional theory of church organization, which may be considered rather like the diagram on the facing page.

And whatever the historical doctrines that are supposed to be central in Presbyterian, Methodist, or Baptist traditions, this idea of first-class and second-class Christians is often as strong among them as among Episcopalians, Lutherans, or even Roman Catholics. As Bishop Stephen Baynes wrote in the London *Church Times* in February, 1961: "There is nobody stuffier than a parson who is

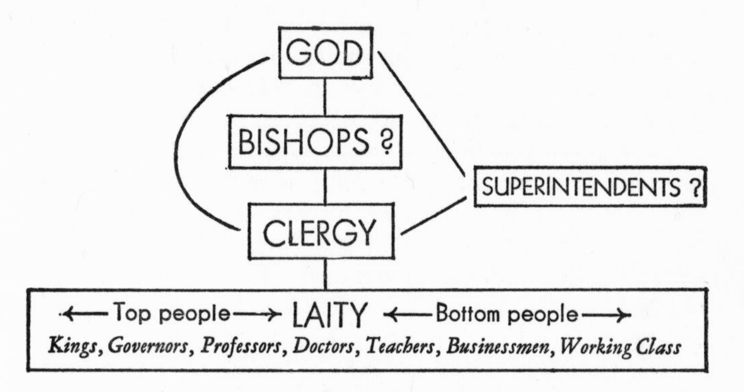

acutely conscious of the privileges of his order, of his monopoly of theological learning, liturgical authority, general sanctity, and so on. The worst of it is that the laity so often believe in all this nonsense, and put the sacred ministry on a pedestal, until they feel that the only way a man can serve God is by being ordained."

Very, very few communities of Christians have avoided such distinctions. We should mention here with great respect the fundamental equality of calling which is found in the beliefs of the Society of Friends (Quakers).

It is one of the exciting facts of the twentieth century that, for a number of reasons, the whole church of God is beginning to rediscover the true doctrine of the laity — something as different from the diagram above as good wine is from methylated spirits. And we mean *exciting,* for this discovery can make our churches lively, revolutionary, human groups again.

A great many historical factors have helped to drive God's people to this painful new thinking — among them, admittedly, a shortage of clergy (which may be truly providential), but also the wonderful growth of secular knowledge and of education for lay people. It was inevitable that the "clergy" should run the medieval churches, because practically every educated man was in "orders" of some kind or another. This was true for most of the important officials and clerks — who were "clerks in holy orders" (which is still the official description for Anglican priests).

For the last two hundred years, education and leadership have not at all been the monopoly of men "in orders," and there has at last been a chance for Christian people to work out a satisfactory doctrine of the laity, and of their daily duties in an industrial society far removed from the traditional peasant life of the European village. In the last twenty years, all this has begun to jell together.

The essence of the matter is to be found in the Old Testament idea of the children of Israel, that priests and prophets and people are *all together* the people of God—an idea that is taken over and developed in the New Testament, and particularly by Paul, as the "church." For to the early Christians the church was not a building around the corner (after all, they met in one another's houses), nor was it a denomination (Christians argued together from the very earliest months, but they were not yet divided as we are), nor was it the clergy, with some kind of "top clergy" controlling things. They would tell us that the church means *people*, people like themselves, the people of God, a community, a fellowship. The local church was the fellowship of Christians meeting in X or Y's house, but the whole church was the fellowship of *all* Christian people — already spread about the ancient world in Jerusalem, in Antioch, in Corinth, and in Rome itself. These were the *"laos"* (this is the Greek word from which our word "laity" is said to come, though there are learned arguments about this among the experts). People like these — including the carpenters, the housewives, and some exceedingly doubtful characters — are together the people of God, the body of Christ. Paul's teaching about this (which can be found in Rom., ch. 12, Eph., ch. 4, and I Cor., ch. 12) has in the Authorized Version been almost incomprehensible to many Christian people. It has been magnificently recovered for us by J. B. Phillips, in his colloquial translation *Letters to Young Churches.* And in his version perhaps more clearly than anywhere else we can see the true doctrine of the laity as the whole people of God in *partnership* together — with no divisions into first class or second class or any other class. For instance, Paul writes in Rom., ch. 12: "Don't cherish exaggerated ideas of yourself or your importance, but try to have a sane estimate of your capabilities by the light of the faith that God has given to you all. For just as you have many members in one physical body and those members differ in their functions, so we, though many in number, comprise one Body in Christ and are all members of one another. Through the grace of God we have different gifts. If our gift is preaching, let us preach to the limit of our vision. If it is serving others let us concentrate on our service: if it is teaching let us give all we have to our teaching; and if our gift be the stimulating of the faith of others let us set ourselves to it. Let the man who is called to give, give freely; let the man who wields authority think of his responsibility; and let the sick visitor do his job cheerfully.

"Let us have no imitation Christian love. Let us have a genuine break with evil and a real devotion to good. Let us have real warm affection for one another as between brothers, and a willingness to let the other man have the credit. Let us not allow slackness to spoil our work and let us keep the fires of the spirit burning, as we do our work for God. Base your happiness on your hope in Christ. When trials come endure them patiently: steadfastly maintain the habit of prayer. Give freely to fellow-Christians in want, never grudging a meal or a bed to those who need them. And as for those who try to make your life a misery, bless them. Don't curse, bless. Share the happiness of those who are happy, and the sorrow of those who are sad. Live in harmony with each other. Don't become snobbish but take a real interest in ordinary people. Don't become set in your own opinions. Don't pay back a bad turn by a bad turn, to *anyone.* Don't say 'it doesn't matter what people think,' but see that your public behaviour is above criticism. As far as your responsibility goes, live at peace with everyone."

There is, then, no essential distinction between clergy and laity, between skilled and unskilled, well educated and little educated, white and black, male and female, Jews and Gentiles, "top" and "bottom" people. The true New Testament picture can be indicated by a second diagram, which puts the clergy and everybody else in a fundamental equality under God:

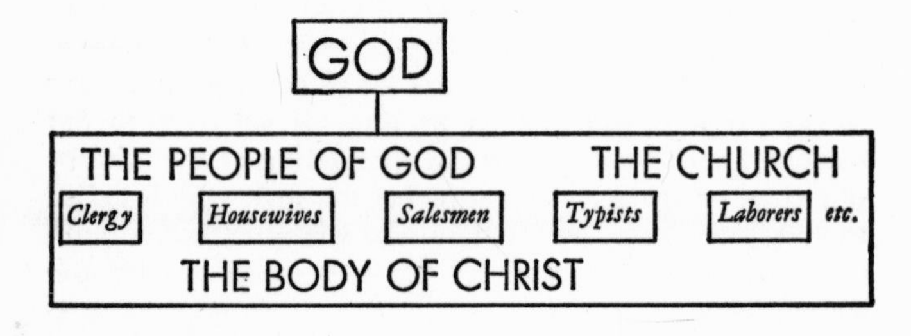

It is literally correct, therefore, to say that all *clergy*—of any type—are part of the "laity," the *laos,* the people of God. If this book is not to become intolerably confusing, we shall have to keep on using the words "clergy" and "laity" in their ordinary English meaning; but it is essential to emphasize the point here that there is no fundamental difference in calling between an archbishop and his chauffeur, between a President and a parish minister—providing they are both in each case faithful and committed Christians. In New Testament jargon, we are all called to be "saints"—not in the stained-glass window sense, but in the sense of being human beings so sanctified and strengthened and enlivened by God's Spirit (there is nothing sanctimonious about true Christian living) that we really can show God's love to his world. And, let it be emphasized once again, a cleaning woman may show God's love better than a tycoon, a copy boy better than an editor, a schoolgirl better than her teacher. There is a basic *equality of calling* among all God's people; we are all saints and sinners together. As Canon Edward Patey said to a technical college teachers' group at Coventry in 1961: "All orders are holy. Plumbers are as much in holy orders as the clergy, serving God and their fellows. . . . Electricians, parkkeepers, doctors and typists are all working as much with the things of God as the priest with the sacrament."

Or as Hans-Ruedi Weber has written in his booklet, *Salty Christians* (The Seabury Press, Inc.): "Too often the clergy undertake to fulfil by themselves the ministry of the Church. And too often the laity delegate their ministry to one man—the clergyman. This 'one man show' is deeply unbiblical. Too many clergy and other Church workers fail to fulfil—or even to see—their main, specific function: the equipment of 'saints' for the ministry.

"Christ does not grant special gifts only to men and women who are full-time, lifetime employees of the Church. All the people of God share in Christ's ministry in and to the world, on the front lines. But the work of front-line soldiers belongs especially to laymen, who spend most of their waking hours in social, political, economic, and cultural areas where the decisive battles of faith are being fought."

No doubt, the clergyman may be chosen by God for certain important functions in the church; and for these functions he is "ordained" in one way or another. Hans-Ruedi Weber continues: "The clergy, with other professional Church workers, have a particular responsibility—to nourish, equip, help, and sustain the laity for their ministry."

Different churches differ very seriously indeed about what kind of "grace" and authority is conferred by different kinds of ordination, but all Christians would readily admit that for these functions a parson deserves the respect and support of the laity. What is, however, of the first importance (and this is increasingly admitted by all kinds of theologians, from Roman Catholic to Baptist) is that lay people are *also* chosen by God to perform other functions in his church, and that for these they too may receive "grace" and authority and the strength of his Spirit. Indeed, there are energetic discussions going on now in the Church of England about whether confirmation might become more obviously some kind of "ordination" of the laity for adult life under God: other churches which have a clear ceremony for admission to full church membership are a step or two ahead here.

This insistence that *all* God's people are chosen, and *all* are offered the grace, the strength, and the guidance of God's Holy Spirit, is all the more important when we consider the different functions of God's church. We have already said that the church was in New Testament times a fellowship of people, not a building and not a group of clergy. And this fellowship Christians do achieve today, particularly perhaps in some suburban churches—and preeminently in the United States. St. Exurbanite's is a fine fellowship—indeed a cozy club of a fellowship, moving from summer tennis to autumn barbecue, and from youth dances to old folks' film shows. And yet, though all these may be worthy and admirably run social groups, we have no hesitation in saying that a fellowship which consists *only* in doing such things together is quite damnable—indeed, it is already damned, or condemned, by all that the New Testament has to tell us about Christian fellowship together.

For the people of God are meant to show God's love to his world, not to enjoy it quietly in a cozy group on their own. They are meant to be the body of Christ—the *embodiment* of Christ's love and compassion toward the world;

and he had terrifying things to say about people who cared for their own comforts—and the welfare of their precious little souls—before the desperate needs of people outside the circle of the church community. God's Holy Spirit is given to his people, not for the running of a "happy fellowship" of Sunday and week-night evening activities, but for the agonizing work of serving—"ministering to" (it's the same word in Greek) the needs of others.

As Dr. von Thadden, president of the German Kirchentag, or Lay Congress, said in his message to the Scottish Kirk Week held at Ayr in August, 1962: "We must learn to serve the *world* better. We must have the courage to come out from our comfortable domestic lives and bring our faith into the dangerous, confusing, and yet exciting life of the world outside the grey walls of our church buildings. And we must have the courage to question much that does go on within these church buildings. To what extent do our Sunday services, our religious jargon, our methods of Bible study, our cozy spirit of fellowship, indicate to the outsider that we are a kind of private religious club (at which he will not be very welcome)? And to what extent does our worship and our church life together offer him a clear message of God's forgiveness and God's concern for his daily life in the factory, the office or the farm? So often a local church seems to exist for the sake of its members, rather than for the people in the streets around. We need the courage to take our Faith outside."

Dr. von Thadden's words are echoed by an article that appeared in the *Presbyterian Outlook,* of Richmond, Virginia, in November, 1961. It was by Robert W. Spike, who wrote: "Christians may go on saying creeds and singing hymns and trying to work out some little niche for religion in their personal lives. But all this is so much nostalgic hogwash if the excitement of confessing Christ as Lord and Savior does not take hold of a man's mind and heart. To be a Christian in any age is to be fully a man—a creature of

God, not isolated and sterilized by your religion, but responsive as a whole human being to the times and the people among whom you are set. It means further to take a chance, to be experimental, to laugh at fate and cry with compassion, to work . . . and to play."

The Bishop of Woolwich, Dr. John Robinson, sums it all up admirably in one of the passages in his paperback *Honest to God* which has not had the attention it deserves: "That Christianity should be equated in the public mind, inside as well as outside the Church, with 'organised religion' merely shows how far we have departed from the New Testament. For the last thing the Church exists to be is an organisation for the religious. Its charter is to be the servant of the world."

It means also that we must *listen*. We are now becoming accustomed to the truth that church people, and indeed Christians, do not have a monopoly of God's truth and that we must all learn to listen to what God is saying to us through non-Christians. As Dr. Visser 't Hooft, General Secretary of the World Council of Churches, said at the 150th anniversary celebrations of Princeton Theological Seminary, in May, 1962, "In some cases agnostics or humanists represent a conception of man that is closer to the Christian view than that of superstitious cults." And we entirely agree with Bishop Ambrose Reeves, formerly Bishop of Johannesburg and now General Secretary of the British Student Christian Movement, when he said in January, 1963: "I have the impression that too often Christians imagine as it were that they hold God in their hands, and that they've got to go to the people who haven't got God and hand him to them. I believe that . . . the type of evangelism which we may find fruitful is where we can go and remember that Christ is already at work in these 'Godless' people."

Or as Ernest Southcott, Provost of Southwark Cathedral, South London, wrote in *Item* in March, 1963: "If I speak from my own experience, I have learnt so much of how God works in the world from people who never clock in to a church service. Yet so often we give the impression that we know all the answers. In fact, we've got a great deal to learn."

For this work of listening, of talking with people instead of at them, of getting to know people in their everyday routine and their local surroundings, the Christian layman is very often God's essential agent. He is called not merely to venture into the world outside the church—that, after all, is where he lives, and works and spends his wages—as to enter cheerfully and dangerously into the spirit and argument and style of modern life—and to find his Lord there before him.

Now, it may very well be that this will include a great deal of Christian activity which is not best done by any type of clergyman. It is quite clear, for instance, that many family doctors have a "pastoral" function of compassion and care for their patients which no clergy can or would wish to take from them; and it is probably true to say that most Christians, including most clergy, would recognize this, and understand that a Christian doctor may be called by God to show his love to the world in his vocation and calling. It is not yet so clear as it ought to be that a mother down the street, or a personnel officer in the plant (or a shop steward with whom he is often arguing), may be equally called by God to be the embodiment of Christ in their particular situation and calling. There was a great deal of controversy when at the Munich Kirchentag, in 1959, Pastor Horst Symanowski said to an audience of lay people, "You are God's pastors and priests in your factories"; but he was right. So was Tom Chapman, industrial liaison officer of the Church of England, when he said at the Bristol Congress of the Student Christian Movement in January, 1963, "A shop steward is very much like a parish priest on a factory floor." All God's people are called to be "saints," to be priests, and prophets, and administrators, and washers of other people's feet; and though obviously we will specialize in our main job in life, none of us can claim the exclusive right to be God's representatives anywhere (or the right to shelve our responsibilities by saying: "He can do it: he's the priest,"—or the vestryman, or the elder, or what have you). In fact, the different gifts of the Spirit are in different people in different degrees. Some Christians are much better at being priests than being administrators—and though they have some administrating to do, they will probably be called to be ordained clergy. Some others are much better at being administrators, and they will probably find God calls them to be civil servants or tycoons—though they will have some priestly functions too.

We must add here that there is an important though not absolute distinction between the "worldly" and the "churchy" laity. The first, which for convenience we may label type "A," have their main interests in the world outside the church buildings, in their careers, in trade, in teaching, in local or national politics, in different voluntary (but not church) organizations such as Rotary or the Woman's Club, and above all, in their home and family life. This means that their ways of serving God will also be mainly in these "worldly" preoccupations. The "churchy" laity, whom we will call laity type "B," and who are a very small percentage indeed of the whole church of God—almost as small as the clergy—are the "good" laity, always around the church premises, having somehow the time for a great range of church work, and to the amazement and reluctant admiration of their fellow laymen, actually finding that their main interest in life centers on their church and its organization. They are keen lay preachers, Sunday school teachers, fund raisers, church officers, and the like. Laity type "B" are invaluable in the running of many churches and we hope in Chapters 7 and 10 to say something about their particular responsibilities and need for training; but we must emphasize the fact that they are only a small minority of God's people, and certainly not the only ones who are serving him faithfully and wholeheartedly.

We have then in this chapter refused to admit a fundamental difference between Christian clergy and Christian laity; but we have readily accepted a difference in function, within the whole body of Christ, between clergy, "worldly" laity type "A" and "churchy" laity type "B." One other way of classifying God's laity is more common than it ought to be; and we would wish to repudiate it energetically. It is often implied, or still worse assumed, that the ones who matter are the well-educated ones, the ones who have or who will have "responsibility"—in British jargon, the "grammar school types." The ones who don't matter so much are those who drop out of high school or college courses. Of course, two hundred years of comparative failure to touch the town working-class populations (as Bishop E. R. Wickham has pointed out) have made us predominantly a middle-class church in Britain—with the conspicuous exception of the Roman Catholics. There is a grave danger that the new moves to train the laity may result in a great many books, and conferences, and courses only suitable for people with good college board grades. We must believe that God cares equally for his truck drivers as for his Harvard professors, for his people who serve in Woolworth's as for his people who design TV commercials; and we must believe this enough to work out methods of training for *ordinary* church members, techniques practical and concrete enough to serve their needs. There is no Ph.D. required for saintliness.

2. *The Developing Church*

So when we talk about the laity we are talking about the church: the whole church and nothing but the church. And we rarely talk about the whole church. When we discuss worship or theology or evangelism we are, of course, also discussing the church but only one aspect of it. We are looking at the church in a particular way. Perhaps we think that when we discuss the laity we are looking at the church in yet another particular way. And perhaps we think it is a new way, a bit odd: interesting but off-center. But the laity is not just another aspect of the church which has been rather neglected. Nor is it just a part of the church—the underdeveloped, underprivileged part of the ecclesiastical world, now stirring with awkward demands. As we have seen in the previous chapter, the laity, strictly, is not a part of the church at all. It is the whole church. It is all the members of the church, the whole people of God.

This is not how we have been taught to think of the church. We have not thought of the church as people. We have thought of the church as an institution to which people belong; which needs people to serve and support it. Or we think of the church as the preserver of doctrine and the container of the gospel, to save people through the truth, and needing its special servants to understand and expound this truth. Certainly we think of the history of the church as the account of how the church has been organized, disorganized, and reorganized. We have seen it as the story of an institution, or we have thought of it as the record of what the councils of the church have decided and of the doctrines that the church has taught. At its most picturesque and personal, it tells how the heroes and martyrs of the church have striven and suffered but always for the defense of the institution or for the sake of the doctrine.

There is another story of the church, the hidden history of how all those who make up the body of the church, the one body that stretches in personal contact right back to Jesus and the men he called, have lived and failed, have loved and suffered. This is the real living history of the church, the story of innumerable men and women, of priests and others, alike. It is the record of unknown men and women rather than of those whose names are remembered. So in a sense the story can never be told, for when a Christian steps into history he seems to cease to be just a member of the church; he becomes a hero or a saint, a theologian or a heretic. But this hidden story tells of the true achievement. It is the saving work of Christ. This is the church more truly than in its doctrine and in its institutions.

The mystery of the church is simply that it is people. It is a divine society, not because of an infallible doctrine or an incorruptible organization, but because Jesus called men to follow him, and still does. It is not a religious society. It is a lay society because it is made up of the men and women Jesus calls.

And it is this that makes the church unique. There is nothing in the great religions of the world with which you can compare the church. There is, for instance, no body of Buddhists which you can call the Buddhist Church. Buddhism is a religion and a man becomes a Buddhist by renouncing the world and becoming a Buddhist priest. He can, of course, declare that he accepts Buddhist teaching. But this is his private affair. There is no body to which he belongs. Christianity is something quite different. If that is religious, this is lay. It is lay because it is essentially made up of people. It is secular because it is sent into this world of today at this time.

The only other societies with which Christianity can be compared at all are Judaism, Islam, and communism, because they share a common root in the Old Testament. They take space and time seriously. They see a meaning in the material world and a purpose in man's history.

It is because of the fundamental beliefs of the Christian faith that we can say, "I believe in God . . . and in the church." We can say we believe in this body of men and women, this lay and secular society, as the creation of God and the body of Christ, because of our basic belief in God's creation of the world and in his redemption of the world in Jesus Christ. Because God is from the beginning at work in his world, because, in the life and death and resurrection of Jesus Christ, he brought his creation to a new stage and in terms of a man, a human being, because his creative work still goes on through his Spirit in men and in the world—because of this fundamental belief we know that the church is the mystery of God's creation: a church made up of men and women, the only true lay, secular society, the herald and the instrument of God's purpose for all mankind.

This high picture of the church as the body of Christ in the world, with all its members called to a united service in that body, is the picture painted for us in the New Testament, especially and most vividly by Paul. It has no place for the division of its members into "clerical" and "lay." It is a picture of which we have ever to be reminded and which we must try to express in terms of the world in which we live today. Our difficulty is that the words we now have to use express division and we have no words to express unity. Even the word "church" causes confusion; its uses are so many and its interpretations so diverse. The common words that the Bible uses—words like "people," "men," "new"—have lost content, and special words like "laity" have acquired an even more specialized meaning.

We have referred to the ordinary, secular meaning of the word "lay" as "uneducated," "uninformed," "amateur." There is also the religious meaning that developed when the church in the Middle Ages became, in the sharp words of Dr. Mascall, "almost completely clericalised." And this meaning is entirely negative: someone who is not ordained. So today the use of the words "lay," "layman," "laity" conjures up in the minds of many people the picture of uneducated amateurs demanding their place and their say in the affairs of the church. They feel somehow that this kind of democratic upsurge is out of place in a society that has only one Head.

And it is not enough to paint in simple, glowing colors the picture of the prototype of the church as we find it in the New Testament before the church became inextricably involved in the affairs of the world. We have to see how the church has been the people of God, and how the "laity" in its more limited sense has fared.

Where do we begin? We can go back to the birth of Jesus, to the call of Abraham, to the creation of the world, but when we consider the church we begin with the fact that Jesus called men to follow him and that from among these disciples he chose some, the Twelve, to be with him and to go out to preach the Kingdom and heal the sick. We can discuss for as long as we like the question, When did the church come into existence? At the call of the first disciples? At the commissioning of the Twelve? At Pentecost? We'll never get a categorical answer. "The ministry of Jesus," wrote T. W. Manson, "is the kingdom of God spelt out in human terms." So must the church be the Kingdom of God spelled out in human terms, for it is the life of men living in Christ that constitutes the church.

The disciples had to be with Jesus, every day and all the day, so that they should not think that what made them the church was a theology that they could teach to men, but should know that it was a life which they shared and into which men could be brought. This was why, when Jesus sent them out two by two, he did not take pains to see that they had got the doctrine right, as we would have done, but was concerned that they should not change their style of living by taking money and a change of clothing and looking around for the best hospitality.

It was only after the resurrection that they knew for themselves the freedom of the life that he had given to them. They continued to live the life they had started with him, only now they knew that it was their life, and they knew that their life was in him.

The words that Jesus used to describe this life of himself and his church were biological rather than institutional. He spoke of seed and of the miracle of growth and of the harvest; of the family and of men's dependence on other men and on things. Words familiar to us and essential to our thinking about the church—words like "clergy" and "laity" and "worship"—were not needed. The only word of this kind which he used and which we still use is the word "minister." But it is never used to describe status or function. It carries always the meaning of the verb "to serve," with behind it the picture of the servant, the willing slave. It was in these terms that he described the life he lived—and the life of his men.

This picture is filled out in the description of the church in The Acts and in the epistles. The gifts given to the church and manifest in all its members were gifts of service—or ministry. Still the language was biological and not institutional. The body was the body of the flesh, not the body politic.

But even when this short period of primitive simplicity was over, and developing life demanded some organized structures, the church existed for three hundred years—and these certainly not the least creative in its history—without certain things that we now take for granted as essential for the existence of the church. It is as well to remember this, to remind us that the church in essence is people and not an institution.

First, the church had no ecclesiastical buildings—no churches. We are so accustomed to the church's having its own buildings for worship and meeting that we find it practically impossible to imagine the church without them. For us the picture conjured up by the very word "church" is that of the parish church in the center of the village, or of spires and towers rising above the houses of the town. The church building enshrines the history of our country and is the guardian of family, local, and national memories. The church building in city streets speaks of worship, quiet, and retreat. Without these buildings there would be no bells to remind us of the passing of time. The building holds so essential a place in our daily life and in our thinking about the church that when we speak of a new housing area as being churchless, we do not mean that there are no Christians in it but that there is no specific building in which they can meet.

It is well to remember that neither Paul nor any of the apostles ever "went to church." They never saw and probably never imagined a building built and set apart exclusively for Christian worship. The only temples they talked about were the Temple in Jerusalem that Jesus said would be destroyed, and the temple that God was building in the world, whose stones were men. It would have seemed odd to them that their names should be most widely perpetuated in buildings—St. Paul's, St. Peter's, St. Thomas' and all the rest. For them the church was the people to whom they belonged or to whom they wrote, not the building in which they met. The local church was the people meeting in someone's house: the church in the house of Priscilla and Aquila (Rom. 16:5; I Cor. 16:19), the church in the house of Nymphas (Col. 4:15) or in the house of Philemon.

This meeting in an ordinary secular house must have given to men a quite different picture of the church from that which is given by our exclusively religious buildings. The house was just the ordinary living quarters of a household. There is no word in Hebrew or Greek for "family." It is of the house and not of the family that the Bible speaks—the building where people live together and in which the ordinary activities of secular life go on.

A house is a place where people live. It is not really a place where people meet, for meeting implies coming and going. A house is where people stay and eat and sleep and gossip, and enjoy themselves, and do nothing in particular. And in those days it was also the place where people did their daily work. So the Christians in Rome and Corinth and Colossae did not meet in the houses of Priscilla and Aquila and of Nymphas and Philemon for worship only. Many lived there, for the Roman household was large, and many of the others would spend most of their free time there. As we know from Paul's letters they met regularly for meals. They met for gossip and indulged in quite a bit of scandal. They met to read and discuss Paul's letters. They met to entertain strangers and to hear what they had to say. Paul's letters to the Corinthians show what the church at Corinth talked about—local scandals, food, going to law, the relation of the sexes, buying and selling, the relationship of master and slave, of old and young. In this secular setting worship would have point and the meaning of the faith would come alive. Inevitably as time passed and numbers increased and a more settled pattern developed, rooms would be set apart and furnished for worship but they remained imbedded in the lay, secular life of the house.

Secondly, the church had no clergy as we think of clergy. There were those who conducted the worship and those who taught and those who prophesied and those who healed the sick and those who looked after the money and those who cared for the poor and the widows. But these were the members of the church, each with his particular gift of service. Inevitably there were those who were outstanding and whose gifts were most prized and most used. And, of course, there were those who could give, and gave, their whole time to the service of the churches. There were the apostles. But there were others who had not this or, seemingly, any other title. There were such men as Barnabas, Mark, and Luke, "the beloved physician." There were others, men and women, who served in much the same way though their travels were not perhaps so constant. There were, for example, Priscilla and Aquila, who traveled widely and yet had a house in which the church met. These itinerant "ministers," to whom the later words "clerical" and "lay" do not apply, supported themselves by the work of their hands, as did Paul and Priscilla and Aquila, or they received living expenses when they stayed in a local church. This seems to have been Peter's practice, perhaps because fishing is not an occupation everywhere practicable. Paul says that, if he had wished, he could have claimed expenses as Peter did, and be accompanied by a wife, as Peter was. But obviously such expenses did not amount to much. They could be likened to what the ox could pick up as it trod the corn (I Cor. 9:9; I Tim. 5:18). There was nothing in the nature of a full-time, professional clergy.

It is doubtful whether there was any full-time professional clergy till the church began to have buildings of its own. It was when the center of the life of the church moved from the houses where men lived to the special places of worship to which men went that the division and distinction between the laity and the clergy became obvious.

Thirdly, there was no professional theological training and therefore no theological seminaries. There was plenty of theological study and discussion. Indeed it could be argued that in no subsequent age was there so much theological education. But it was carried out in the whole body of the church. It was not a specialist study for the training of the professional servants of the church. Paul's letters were not written to be studied by ordinands in seminaries; they were written to be read in church and to be studied by all the members of the church. And sometimes Paul was present to speak himself. And when the meeting place was a hot upper room and men and women met at night because they were at work during the day, when with the heat and the lateness and with the discussion a youth could become so drowsy that he fell from the window, the discussion could have been anything but formal. The discussion may often have seemed abstruse, but there could never have been any question in men's minds as to what Paul was writing or speaking about and to whom he was referring. It was an unruly and chaotic training in theology, but it was open to all and all could contribute. It must have been stretching to the mind and to the imagination.

Doubtless it was in this corporate study and discussion that some men found where their particular ministry lay. Probably they borrowed collections of the sayings and actions of Jesus and Paul's letters and copied them to study by themselves. Or they went off on their travels to hear what others had to say or to find out what kind of discussion went on in other places. But theirs was not a separated, professional study. It was carried on in the midst of the noisy life of the church and was shared by others, merchants, slaves, and women, all of whom made their contribution. It was a theological education for the people of the church—it was lay, not clerical.

And lastly, and to us very strangely, this life which was so fully and truly secular and lay had no "official" place in the surrounding, ordinary, secular life of men. It had no relation, except that of opposition, to what we now call the "establishment."

This is something we find very hard to imagine, much more to understand. For us it is natural and right that the church should have its part to play in the life of society and nation. We feel that the church should know that it has this service and that it should be seen to be fulfilling it. We see the church as called to set an example, to lead, to serve. The lay church of the New Testament and the two following centuries never saw itself in this light. It knew itself as the herald, the earnest, and the instrument of the new ordering of the world which was already manifest in Christ. But so far as society and the state were concerned the church did not "belong." It was a small minority, always under suspicion, often persecuted. To the state it was a puzzle, an irritation, a challenge, and in the end, a rival.

These four things—buildings, clergy, seminaries, and social responsibility with, as the other side of the coin, social respectability—are all things that we take for granted for the church. We cannot conceive of the church's existing without them. If we did not have to raise money to build new buildings and to maintain old ones, if we did not have to train and maintain the clergy and undertake social service in our own country and elsewhere, what would members of the church do? What did the early church do when it did not have to trouble about these things? It converted the Roman Empire.

Of course, we need these things in some form. An organization cannot exist without some kind of structure. The church, no less than the family, needs some kind of institution. But it can be of the flimsiest. The church—and the family—can do without a building. The church—and the family—can live in tents, can be on the move. The church—and the family—can exist without its official leaders. A family still exists when the parents are dead. The church—and the family—can be outcast and outlawed. The only thing without which the church—and the family—

cannot survive is a way of life, a bond of affection, expressed in custom, tradition, and ceremony, which for the church comes from the life that Jesus lived with men. But, though it needs some structure, the church, like the family, is not primarily an institution. It is essentially people living a life together: the people of God living the life of Christ.

This conception of the church is the only one in evidence in the first three centuries of its history. It is to be seen also in the way in which its enemies and outsiders generally refer to the church—as "these men" (Acts 5:35), "unlearned and ignorant men" (ch. 4: 13), "any of this way, whether they were men or women" (ch. 9: 2), "Christians" (ch. 11: 26). They use names that apply to people and not to institutions.

We see this also in the way in which they spoke of themselves—"they that believed," the New Israel, those whom God was building into his new house for the world. If they had thought of themselves as a company apart from and unconcerned with other men, they would more easily have adopted the language of an institution. But they did not so regard themselves. They knew that they belonged to the ordering of a new world. They believed that all men belonged, in the purpose of God, to this new order and therefore to their company, because Jesus was Lord of all and had died for all and had broken down the walls of partition. This conviction of belonging to the one body to which all people must belong, even as rebels, was the spring of their mission and the reason why they were persecuted.

We in the countries of the West have never known a church like this. It is good for us to remember that this was what the church was like in the beginning and is in essence. By the providence of God its picture is enshrined for us forever in the New Testament: to remind us that however necessary institutional structures may be, the church is not primarily an institution but people, by the grace of God, living the life that is in Christ.

But it became an institution, clerical and religious, with buildings, clergy, political responsibilities, and respectability. It became this because the lay life and mission had been successful. The seal of its success was when the Emperor Constantine in 312 recognized Christianity and later adopted it as the religion of the Roman Empire. The church became the great institution which we in the West still know today. The church came to have all the things which we now think of as the rightful possessions and the necessary tools of the church.

Instead of being an illegal minority, the church assumed responsibilities for the life of the world and undertook a supreme part in ordering the lives of men. To express and maintain these responsibilities and duties the church developed an organization: an ecclesiastical service to balance the civil service of the state. Inevitably this was built up on the pattern of the civil organization: in provinces, in cities, and much later, in parishes. And, just as the state was seen and thought of as the emperor, the provincial governors, the officials, and the army and not as the people they ruled, so the church came to be thought of as the clergy and not the people.

But although the actions of the church came quite soon and quite clearly to be thought of as what was done by the clergy and done in ecclesiastical buildings, the division between the clergy and the people was never so clear and simple as this description would seem to imply. There was still the strong, inherited sense of Christians being the people of God. There was also the claim of the civil power that the sword it carried was also the sword of the Lord and it too his servant. This was the ground of the controversies between emperor and pope.

This unresolved quarrel between the bearers of the spiritual and the secular sword, each claiming to be directly the servant of God, ceased to represent in any way the division between clergy and laity when education came to be accepted as the prerogative of the clergy, and all who could read and write were regarded as clerical. The privileges known as "benefit of clergy," which freed a man from the jurisdiction of the civil courts, depended upon the ability to read and write and not upon the fact of ordination. When this happened the laity were indeed in an inferior position, outside the real life of the church.

This was the position of the laity in the later Middle Ages. The layman was outside the worship and the discussion of the church because of his ignorance. If he wanted to have a footing in the life of the church, he had to belong to some religious order—of knighthood or of guild. Yet he was not in the position of the millions of Buddhists whose numbers are in our atlases and encyclopedias but whose names are known to no Buddhist priest, who may be Buddhists in their private thought but are only spectators and intruders in the worship of the temples. The medieval layman was not a cipher like this. He was called to be of the faithful. He was the recipient of the crumbs of grace. He had his place of service and his reward.

The institution, however, had become almost completely clericalized. But it did not continue unchallenged, even by the clergy. The old "lay" life continued and flowered. It flowered in the early monasteries, which were composed mainly of laymen. Continually there were revolts and reforming movements, which were sometimes attempts to find the way of return to New Testament simplicities, sometimes efforts to follow new lines of missionary outreach, and sometimes even ways of finding new freedom for the secular sword. All these movements were essentially anticlerical and, therefore, lay. The last of them—the Reformation—split the institution. The force behind the Reformation was the desire of men, lay members of the church, to find the joy and exercise of their faith in their daily secular lives. They felt that they should be able to live full and effective Christian lives without abandoning their families and occupations and entering a monastery. They were filled with this new desire because they were finding new meaning and satisfaction in their families, in their businesses, and in the education which with the founding of the universities was now open to them. For the first time since the beginning of the Dark Ages there was a kind of secure, peaceful, cultured family life, now that the manor had taken the place of the castle and town life had developed which offered to men new scope for the exercise of art and skill and learning, if also of ambition and greed. Education was no longer the preserve of the clergy. The new universities and grammar schools were for laymen as well as for intending ministers. And the life of the manor house and town house was a threat to the religious orders.

All kinds of other factors were engaged in the coming of the Reformation—economic, political, and theological. But without this desire to see the church as the church of the people and without the conviction of men that they were called to serve God in their secular calling, there would have been no Reformation in the church but only some reforms. So we have the picture of the plowman singing psalms as he plowed, of the merchant serving God at his desk, and of the scholar at his prayers. It is a new layman that has appeared. He is by no means exclusively a Protestant figure. Sir Thomas More, with his family life, his public service, and his private scholarship, is as much the new layman as any Puritan soldier or scholar.

So at the time of the Reformation and for a short time afterward there was the promise of a full lay life in the church again, with laymen leading in service in church and state, with laymen reading and writing theology.

But the promise faded. There was a vigorous lay life in the church so long as economic life found its productive unit in the family and the obedience of a Christian could be adequately expressed in family life, public service, and private morality. But this simple pattern based on a simple agricultural economy did not long survive. New discoveries in science and new developments in industry broke it. Men had to go out of their homes to work. New and larger groupings of men were created in factory and shop and office. A new split appeared. This was not the old one between clergy and laity but a new one between church and society—between what a man heard in church and what he did in the world. The new forms of industrial and economic life developed outside the jurisdiction and outside the concern of the church. A man's Christian obedience was still in the old terms of family life, public service, and private morality. But these, which before had covered the whole of his life, now had to do only with a part—the private, domestic part lived in a man's leisure time. The layman's obedience came to be seen as in the church, not in the world. It had nothing to do with his work and his livelihood. This naturally did not happen at once. Indeed it can be said to have happened fully only in our own day.

The evangelical revival of the eighteenth and early nineteenth centuries rediscovered and revived the Reformation conception of the layman. It did so by converting the man of leisure; by recalling him to an obedience in the old terms of family life, public service, and private morality. Perhaps John Wesley came too early to effect the development of the industrial revolution to any great extent. But if he had come much later, the rich, powerful, leisured class would already have begun to disappear. The great philanthropists of this time all belong to this class. Life for them was bounded by family life, public service, and private morality. Industry never touched their own lives. But politics did. In Britain we commonly think of William Wilberforce as a great philanthropist and for us that word has no political connotation. But Wilberforce was essentially a politician, whose field of operation was the House of Commons. The spring of his actions was his Christian faith, but this meant no holding back from involvement in party politics, from political propaganda, and from the use of all the means that made political action effective.

Why was this not the beginning of a strong tradition of political action by churchmen? We do not mean that the great political figures of the succeeding generations were not Christians. Some undoubtedly were. The famous British prime minister W. E. Gladstone certainly was a great Christian layman. But he seemed to belong to an earlier religious world than his contemporaries. The successors of Wilberforce the politician were the private philanthropists, who inaugurated and supported causes, who had no concern with fundamental economic issues, who feared the workers and thought that nothing could be done about working conditions and wages.

Behind the fear of revolution and the acceptance of the immutability of economic laws was the belief that the obedience of the Christian man was confined to the spheres of family life, public service, and private morality. But now he knew that there was another world outside these spheres. In the Victorian age he still managed to avoid its questions.

So we have the laymen of the last century. These are the men whose names are on the stained-glass windows of our older town and suburban churches. These inscriptions do not mention public service so often as did the monuments of the eighteenth century. Instead they mention philanthropy and service to the church. The Victorian laity did great things in these spheres; spheres that had become much narrower than in the days of Wilberforce, but that seem to us perhaps narrower than they in fact were. For these Victorian men and women had a greatness denied to us—a certain freedom as they moved among men. They were truly lay. They had not become clericalized.

3. *The Frustrated Layman and the Bewildered Parson*

The Victorian age is remote from us today. Perhaps in the church we scarcely realize its remoteness. There is good reason for this. Its trappings are still our familiar surroundings in the church. Many of our church buildings are new. But what goes on in them is based on the pattern of the last century. Our religious imagination is, to a great extent, based on the paintings, the stained-glass windows, and more particularly, the music and the hymns of the church life of the nineteenth century.

And we do not see them as they were. We think of the typical Victorian house as rather dark, overgrown with ivy and overshadowed by trees and bushes. We forget that to the Victorians it was a new house of light stone, and around it light and space and only a few young trees. We do not see its life in its freshness and its brashness, in its confidence and its blindness, in its love of novelty and its fear of change. We think that we belong to it as to an old and confirmed world. We talk about preserving or recovering its manners and its teaching. As if we could!

For it is a world that is in some ways more remote and less intelligible than the world of New Testament times or the world of the Middle Ages. We can never see it clearly, for everything in it is distorted by the haze of inherited memories. The church of the New Testament and after, with its lack of buildings, its absence of professional clergy, and its refusal to have any part in the contemporary "establishment" is so foreign to us and so devoid of any inherited associations that we can imagine it with some clarity just because it is strange. The church of the Middle Ages, with its hierarchy of authority and its conception of a static society, has for us the quality of a dream with the fascination of the unattainable. We can see these patterns of church life because they are different from our familiar pattern and therefore distinct. We think we are familiar with the church of our grandparents and great-grandparents. We fail to notice that their world too is quite a different one from ours.

The immediate setting of our daily lives is radically changed. Our world is no longer the family, the village, or even the nation as it was in our great-grandparents' day. We no longer feel that we are set in clearly defined social units and linked to other people in recognized relationships. The family has no longer the wide but strictly defined boundaries of kin that it had last century. It is not now that wide society of uncles, aunts, and cousins, on whom one had claim and whose claims one recognized, which was for many the limits of their social life. But it covered a wide area. It had the permanence and stability of a life that continued from generation to generation. Today the family in the pattern of parents and their children is a small, temporary unit that survives for one generation and then disappears to be succeeded by the small temporary families of the next generation. The family, therefore, ceases to be for most people the stable, unchanging background of their lives. It has been pared of its wider relationships. A man today has lost the security of feeling that the family is there to fall back upon. He has lost the possible excitement of rebelling against it. The family has become a man's responsibility rather than his support.

In much the same way, the village or the town in which he lives is no longer the self-contained area of a man's actions and interests. A person no longer lives in a little part of the world which he knows as his own, around which he can draw a firm boundary. Instead, men today live in a multitude of ever-changing relationships which they cannot easily define or limit; neither accept as inevitable nor rebel against with conviction. We do not quite know where we belong. We live in one place and work in another. Town and country merge into each other. The smaller unit, of village or parish, is swamped in a larger area. A man is not so very certain what his own background is. He has to choose it or, rather, create it, even as he now chooses his friends rather than accepting his wider family as of old. This sense of being an individual who has to create his own environment and indeed make his family life is new and strange and very bewildering.

And the nation is not the unquestioned certainty that it was to his grandparents. It no longer stands by itself in proud sovereignty. We are involved in relationship with other men with whom we have no bond save our common humanity. Our nationalistic cries are surely the despairing cries of those who know that national independence is outdated. There is a sense in which we have to create a new world and are not at all sure where it begins or where it ends.

G. M. Trevelyan has pointed out that our world has changed more in the last hundred years than it did in the previous thousand. But it is not merely the circumstances of our lives that have changed; it is all that we mean by our "world." The boundaries are now quite undefined, whether we think in terms of domestic or national or international life. Our world is just where we live and is as large as we make it. Men are, therefore, now aware that their Christian obedience can no longer be expressed in terms of family life, public service, and private morality—or, perhaps we should rather say, that these three phrases do not have the simple meanings they used to have. Private morality can no longer be interpreted, as it could have been even a hundred years ago, as having to do with those with whom we have visible personal relationships. We now are uncomfortably aware that it is our attitude and behavior to those outside our private lives that matter most for our world; that the daily work of those divided from us by color, race, and creed makes our life comfortable and secure and that our response to them may decide the chances of our peace. What matters now is our relationship —international, industrial, social, and political—with those with whom we have no personal contact but on whom our life depends. Our old, conventional private morality seems often little more than a code of good manners, pleasant among friends but useful in the world only as it hides a determined purpose. We have lost the self-confidence of the Victorians. We are tempted sometimes to call them, or some of them, sanctimonious or hypocritical. We feel that they did not have the doubting questions and uncertainty of motive that we have. And indeed we may well be surprised at their blindness—as, for instance, their blindness to how they made their money when they were so responsible as to how they spent it. Their self-confidence—and their blindness—was due to their certainty about the limits of the society to which they belonged and about their social relationships. We cannot recover their confidence and their certainty. We are called to find a way of life in utterly different circumstances and we don't know where to look for its plan.

Or perhaps we do. We in the church know where we ought to look. We know that in the life of the church and in our understanding of the faith help is to be found. That is why there have sprung up throughout the world so many experiments in parishes and congregations, so many communities of varying kinds, so many lay training institutes—all of which are seeking to find out how the people of the church should be living in the world today. Some of these are set in the ordinary, ongoing life of the church; some are on the fringe of the church's life; some are right outside. All speak in differing terms of the life of the laity and of their task in the world. All are looking for new forms of obedience, new kinds of training. They all talk, to the mystifying of many others, as if they were searching for a new kind of layman, as if he was not to be found in the church today. Sometimes they talk as if this layman who can see his obedience in the wider terms of the world today was only to be found outside the church; as if the church had become so clericalized that a real layman was hardly to be found in it; or as if he had to be a new creation.

Why is this?

Why, when so many of the people of the church feel this urgent need, are they so helpless to do anything?

Why is there no revolt, no breakthrough, as there was repeatedly in the Middle Ages and finally at the Reformation?

Why are the lay movements inside the church so respectable, so slow, so largely sponsored by the clergy?

Undoubtedly the reason for this paralysis of the church — and in particular for this inactivity of the laity — is our blindness to the world around us, our lack of understanding of the faith and of the resources at our disposal and, when we do have a glimmer of understanding, our pathetic cowardice. Undoubtedly it is a failure of faith and hope and love. But it is also because we do not see the church as the instrument of the action of faith and hope and love. We think of the church as static and above the flux of events. We have inherited a conception of the church as concerned solely with the private and domestic side of life. We have come to think it strange that the church should be actively engaged in, and not merely critically concerned with, the public, political, industrial life of the world. And we have developed a pattern of life, particularly in the local church, which expresses this private, domestic side and excludes all concern with the public aspects of life. The result is that when men are painfully aware of living in a new world and gropingly aware of new demands upon them and even begin to glimpse a new vision of the meaning of the faith, they find themselves set in a pattern of church life that seems to preclude any kind of action.

This pattern of church life has now become so fixed, and has been fixed now for so long a time, that men do not realize that it is relatively new, that there have in the past been other patterns and that members of the church have not always been so frustrated as they are today. The layman has become clericalized in a way unknown in any previous age. The minister is more bewildered and uncertain of his job than in any previous age.

This has happened quite unconsciously through the development of this new pattern of life in the local church. The pattern is common throughout the industrialized parts of Western Europe and of America but is foreign to the church in Asia and Africa, even though Western missionaries have done their best to introduce it. It is common to all denominations, whatever their theology and whatever their doctrine of the church. Study the parish magazines or bulletins of all the churches you know. Don't look at the material supplied by a central agency, ecclesiastical or otherwise. Look at what is particular and local — the notices of meetings and events in the parish. Or listen to the announcements of forthcoming events given out in church on Sunday. Or study the notice boards outside the church, which announce regular weekly events. It does not matter whether the churches be Baptist or Episcopalian, Methodist or Presbyterian, their notices will be much the same, because their way of life is much the same. They may announce the events under different names but they are of the same things — women's meetings, men's meetings, youth organizations.

Many people criticize this pattern because they find it inadequate and unsatisfying. But they don't do anything to change it because they think this is the unchanging and unchangeable way of church life. *We forget that it is comparatively recent.* In the remoter rural areas, in the far north of Scotland for instance, you will still find parishes that do not know this pattern, where there is no church hall because there are never any week-night meetings for young people or adults or any Sunday school. It is not, as visitors sometimes think, that church life has decayed and nothing is left. It is that these parishes have preserved the pattern of church life that was set up in England and Scotland at the Reformation and continued for over two hundred years; when the church building was open only on Sunday, for the Word and Sacrament, because daily worship was family prayers and the life of the church was in the homes of the people.

The only possible name to give to this common, now almost universal, pattern of church life in Britain today is "congregational." It is the life that congregates around the church building. We do not use the word here with any reference to the order of church government of the Independents or Congregationalists as we now call them. Nor has it any reference to the older use of the word "congregation" by the Scots Reformers. They spoke in the sixteenth century of the landowners who upheld the Reformation as "the Lords of the Congregation." They used it sometimes in the sense of the "parish," as on the Communion plate of Govan Old Parish dated 1793 and inscribed "Govan Congregation." Both of these uses were employed to emphasize that the church was the people. The word is used here because it is the best description of what is now our common pattern of church life, a life which *congregates* in the church building on week-nights as on Sunday.

This congregational pattern might be called the indigenous pattern of American church life, for from the earliest days churches in America were voluntary associations of lay people rather than institutions imposed from above. In Britain the congregational pattern began to appear only a hundred and fifty years ago and became established in the towns a hundred years ago. It was the means by which the church met the appalling problem caused by the influx of men, women, and children from the rural areas into the new industrial towns in search of work. When the old family life broke down, the church had to find some other pattern of Christian living for its people.

The church began where the need was most obvious—in the provision of some kind of education for children. The Sunday school was the pioneer of the new pattern of church life. The Sunday school made necessary the building of church halls, and it was followed by the provision of opportunities for recreation and religious instruction for other and older sections of the depressed, industrial community. So there were classes and recreational activities for young men, and agencies for the relief of those deprived of the support of family life.

We should note two things about the beginning of this new kind of church life, for they are difficult for us now to appreciate.

First, the impetus to these new ventures did not come from the courts of the church or from its leaders or from the majority of the members of local churches. These new movements were advocated and pioneered by private societies, often national and nondenominational in their scope. They met a good deal of resistance in the church, where they were regarded as an unwelcome and unnecessary intrusion into the centuries-old pattern of Sunday worship and family life.

Second, these movements, whether essentially philanthropic as was the early Sunday school movement or essentially evangelistic as in the case of the foreign missionary societies—and all of them lay-based rather than clerically-based—were for *other people.* They were for the benefit of those outside the church. Sunday schools were not started to teach the children of the church. They were for those who had not the benefit of the family life of the church. Indeed even at the beginning of this century the good church member did not send his children to Sunday school, as this would indicate that his home was without Christian teaching. Nor would he have gone to a week-night meeting except to the session, or other court of the church, nor his wife to anything save to the Dorcas Society to sew clothes for the poor or the heathen. Meetngs in the church halls were essentially for those outside or for the depressed in the church.

To us today this seems a parody of the life of a congregation. Since the First World War there has been a shift of direction: from a philanthropic concern with those outside to a direct concern with the obedience of those inside. This change has demanded a revolution in attitude. And, on the face of it, it may seem to be a turning of the clock back. Surely it was better to be concerned with the relief of the needy in the society round about, even if it was done patronizingly, and with the evangelization of the rest of the world, even if the activity of the congregation was limited to raising money to get other people to do the work, than to be occupied with dances and table tennis and debates.

The trouble has been, not that we are beginning to be concerned with the weekday life of members of the church, but that we have kept the program but not the passion of a previous age. Our congregational activities are still concerned with religious instruction, but now for the children of the church, and with leisure-time activities, but no longer for those who have no other opportunity. Religious instruction of the young must always be the duty of the church and there is a place for recreation for those who share a common life. But, on turning its attention to the life of its own members, the church has not begun realistically to deal with the full life of its members, with the problems and anxieties of adult life, with the questions that arise for a man in his job or that confront men and women together in their political life in community and nation. There are, of course, movements of advance in innumerable places. There is certainly grave dissatisfaction in most places with the inadequacy of congregational life. Wherever discussion on this question takes place, there is agreement that the congregation must develop from the nursery school stage at which it seems stuck at the moment to some kind of adult, responsible life. But advance is blocked by one thing.

Without deliberate planning and certainly without any nefarious scheming on the part of the clergy, the congregation has developed a structure that depends entirely on the minister. The life of the congregation has grown up around him and depends on him and it does not matter whether he is called priest or pastor, rector or minister. His central position has determined the organizations and activities of the congregation and the nature of its piety. This is seen as so natural that most people will say that it is only right; that this is why you have ministers at all; that this is their job; for this they are trained. But for all that, this is what is crippling the life of the church.

The congregational pattern of church life is dependent on the minister in a way unknown before this century. The life of the church of the first three centuries was not dependent on the professional ministry. The lay life of the church in the later Middle Ages was so abandoned and bereft of spiritual content that the laity rose in revolt. The life of the Reformation Church was expressed in the family and depended on the father of the family rather than on the minister.

In the development of the congregational pattern of church life the minister has changed from being the one ordained to the ministry of Word and Sacrament to being in addition the director of the work and activities of a congregation. In the beginning of the development of this new pattern of Christian living no experiment was possible without the approval and enthusiasm of the minister, and it was mainly by the vision and drive of the clergy that congregational life developed with its wide variety of activities and its philanthropic and evangelistic zeal. While we now begin to see the weakness of the pattern, we have to remember its past achievement in keeping its so-called middle class in the church (at the cost of making the church middle class. But how much worse off we would have been if the middle class were not in!), in giving to the men of the last century a desire for service and a means of expressing it, and by making them realize that the Christian life was still a corporate thing. But now the chance of any new development is made impossible because of the central position of the minister. Any growth into a new and wider range of interests and activities is prevented by the fact that the minister must have oversight and control of all the life and activities of his congregation. There is a limit to the number of people with whom one man can work and to the number of activities he can control. And today in most active churches the minister has been pushed beyond that limit. So no new development is easy.

This limiting factor is clearly to be seen in any local church. If you visit two churches, each with a single minister, but the one with two thousand members and the other with five hundred, you would expect to find four times as many in the various organizations — for youth, for women, for men — in the larger church than in the smaller. But you never do. They are generally much the same. Where the church has a larger staff there are many more active members. But their number depends not on the size of the congregation but on the size of the staff. It depends on the minister. And though administrative ability varies, there seems to be a definite limit to the number of persons with whom one man can have effective relations in work, and a limit to the number of activities over which he can have effective relations in work, and a limit to the number of activities over which he can have effective oversight. Experience of industry (and of the army) would indicate that the number of persons with whom a man can work responsibly is very small. In industry the number of members of staff that a senior manager can effectively supervise is said to be seven. The number of persons with whom a man can have some personal relationship is about two hundred. This is the reason for the move toward the small factory unit as being more efficient.

The minister is not running a factory, but his position in the local church is not unlike that of the managing director. His relationship with his people is not confined to one activity of their lives but has to do with the whole range of their anxieties and hopes. On the other hand, he is not with them five days a week for eight hours a day. He sees them intermittently in their leisure time. It would therefore seem that the number with whom he can have personal contact would be much smaller than in the case of a factory manager.

Some may say that this comparison of the church with the organization of industry is wrong and unfortunate. They may say that the relationship of the minister to his people is quite different. The purpose of his relationship is indeed quite different, but is the fact of the present organization of the church not surprisingly parallel — at least with inefficient industry? Is there not much that the church can learn from industry? Would we not learn that the congregation cannot be run in dependence on one man — at least if we look for development and results?

This dependence of the local church on one man is generally emphasized by the organization of the church. The parish minister, the rector, the pastor of the congregation — whatever name you give him — is held to be responsible for the welfare of those committed to his charge. This is interpreted as an individual, personal responsibility. It is his responsibility to God — but then we are all responsible to God for our brothers. He is responsible to his superior — be it church court or bishop. Where his office is a legal possession, his responsibility is reinforced by his sense of a privilege to be defended. However he sees his task, whether he sees it mainly in terms of liturgy and prayer or of the pastoral care of his people, he knows that he must be aware of and approve all that goes on in his church and that he must bear the responsibility. The last thing he wants to have to admit is that something has been going on among his people of which he knows nothing. He is afraid of anything happening of which he would not approve. He knows that it is he who will have to bear the criticism. Ignorance will not be taken as an excuse. It will rather be his condemnation: he should have known what was going on in his church. However able the minister, however streamlined his organization, there is a limit to what one man can know and do. This limit has been the limit of a church's development in work and witness. And often even this limit is not reached. It is safer to see that nothing new or open to question is allowed to happen — safest of all to make sure that nothing happens.

This is an ineffective way of running any organization. No factory — no regiment — could survive if conducted on this system of the authoritative rule of one man. For a church which is a body of people called into the life and work of Jesus Christ it is disastrous. Behind this way of thinking is the picture of the minister as a pastor and of the people as his flock. The picture of the pastor goes back to the Old Testament; but those who make much today of the pastoral responsibility of the minister forget that in the Old Testament the shepherd is the model not of the priest but of the ruler, that in Israel there was only one Shepherd and that the sheep of his pasture were men.

The new conception of the minister as the little king of a little kingdom is an affront to the faith and the intelligence of the members of the church and a constant frustration to individuals and groups in the church who want to be more active in their obedience and even to make experiments. The layman comes to feel that the church is ruled by the clergy and that the exercise of his gifts is not to be encouraged. He is perhaps prepared to accept that the central power of the church must be mainly in the hands of those who have been called to the full-time service of the church and he is so mesmerized by the distance, the size, and the authority of such bodies as the Convocation and the General Assembly that he is content that his voice should not be heard. He may feel rebellious and he is privately critical, but it is with the useless rebellion of the one against the many. In the local situation he suffers from a different frustration; the frustration of the powerless many against the one who seems to hold absolute power.

Those laymen who feel that the position is intolerable and that there is no scope for the contribution of their abilities and interests find that there is little they can do but fade out. They may hope for a change when the parson goes. They may set out on the quest for a different kind of church. But in the end they give up and join the huge army of the lapsed.

Those who remain do so because this is what they like, or, if they sometimes wish it were otherwise, they don't imagine it could be. They have never known anything else and have never heard of anything else from their fathers or grandfathers or anyone else. They have been brought up to see their church membership in terms of their relationship to the minister; not in terms of their relationship to their fellow members. "I go to Father Black's Mass." "Pastor White baptized me." Status in the local church is often in terms of this relationship. One of the reasons why a church likes an "attentive" minister and the reason why a visit from the curate is not very highly regarded is this matter of status.

So the "loyal" part of the congregation likes and upholds the centrality of the minister. And however much a minister may strive for other things, he yet likes to feel that he is appreciated. He has lost a great deal of the position he used to have in the community — in his own right as a leader of society. Now, when he has sunk into a social equality with others, he is apt to find the justification of his position in the dependence of others on him. Bishop Lesslie Newbigin, speaking at New Delhi drew attention to the evil that the central position of the foreign missionary still works in the younger churches overseas. He likened it to the desire of the minister at home to be the "prima donna" of his social church. The desire to hold the stage and to shine, not only as a leader of worship but as an organizer or as a pastor to whom people come with their troubles, appeals to a man's ambition — and to the quelling of the inner suspicion that his ministry as a servant should be something different. But does he often suspect that his position is crippling the growth of the church?

For the effect of the solitary, central position of the minister goes farther than the limiting of the number of the members of the local church to those who can have a personal link with the minister. It also determines the kind of activities in which the member of the church engages. The interests, concerns, and activities of a congregation are determined by the interests, concerns, and activities of the minister. If the minister is interested in foreign missions, drama, and table tennis, then these will tend to be the activities of the congregation. If his successor is interested in youth work, relief of refugees, and music, then the interests of the congregation will be found to change to suit. It is taken for granted that the minister should be the arbiter of his church's thoughts and actions. It is thought that it is for this that he has been trained. He is supposed to know what a congregation ought to be doing. So the life of a congregation is often determined by the curriculum of its minister's theological seminary. If the seminary were indeed concerned with the kind of life the laity should be living, there might be something to say for this. But there would still be the same difficulty — that the interests of the minister dictate the activities of the members of the congregation and no new interest or activity is likely to find its place in its life unless it is shared and supported by the minister. It is not strange that the life and activities of the congregations of the church should remain uniform and strangely static.

This centrality of the minister has had another and yet more dangerous result. The minister has been adopted as the pattern and example of the piety of the laity. This is something new. In the Middle Ages, when education was confined to the clergy and when there was a clear distinction between the clergy and the laity, there was no point in telling the layman to copy the monk or priest. The only way he could do so was by going into a monastery and entering the "religious" life. During the Reformation the division between laity and clergy was broken down, or at least the scandal of it. There was seen to be a religious life for the laity. His sphere of Christian obedience was recognized to be in his family and his work. Vocation was interpreted in terms of secular as well as of religious activities. There were the Christian vocations of the king, the soldier, the lawyer, the farmer, just as there was the vocation of the minister. This conception was strongly held until the industrial revolution. In the seventeenth and eighteenth centuries the vicar of an English parish or a Scots parish minister was prepared to teach his parishioners their jobs. He would have told them how they ought to act as soldiers, lawyers, farmers, servants. He would not have expected them to take him as their model, for his vocation was different. He would have regarded such an attitude as a bit of impertinence. He did not think of himself as the exemplar or even as the pastor of a congregation. He knew himself as the minister of the parish: half teacher and half magistrate for all the people. He expected them to do as he told them and felt himself well qualified to tell them what their Christion duty was in their several occupations. Relics of this position still survive. In Britain a minister of religion, of any denomination, is recognized as still having something of a magistrate's authority: he may witness applications for a passport and other documents. In America the houses of Congress have their chaplains. So do the Armed Forces. To these older vocations of lawgiver and soldier the minister is expected to have something to say.

One of the most tragic mistakes in the history of the church was its failure to think out the vocation of men in industry. The church of the Reformation and of the Counter-Reformation believed in the vocation of all Christian men but tragically accepted in fact a division between church and industry. The church never thought out a code of behavior for the millowner and the factory worker as it had thought out a code of behavior for the older occupations. So "business methods" has a different connotation from "professional behavior." The church left the owner and the worker alone insofar as their work was concerned: the owner alone in the use of his power and the worker alone in his powerlessness. All that the church did generally was to teach the owner to be charitable and temperate in the use of his wealth and the worker to be submissive in his poverty. Christian ethics was concerned with how a man spent his money, not with how he made it or failed to make it. The church in this way abandoned any idea of vocation in the ordinary lives of men — at least in the increasingly dominant spheres of industry and commerce. The church continued to speak of vocation in terms of the older professions. The church could describe the doctor, the teacher, the lawyer, and the soldier in terms of service. Those in the newer occupations of industry and commerce were left without guidance as to how they should behave in their work. Christian vocation came, indeed, in the minds of men, to be restricted to the work of the minister and the foreign missionary, while Christian obedience was in terms of their domestic life and their leisure.

So today the member of the church who is in industry, be he employer or employed, shop steward or director, has received from the church no teaching or training as to how he should do his job. He may not be aware that he has received no help, for he has been brought up with the conviction that his faith has nothing to do with his work. He finds that what he hears in church has little relevance to what he does in his job. He is often uncomfortably aware of this, so that he tends not to come to church; or if he continues to come, he is still convinced that Christian teaching does not apply to commerce and industry. This is not to imply that the factory worker, the manager, the shop steward, and the director do not have their codes of behavior or that their standards of behavior are not influenced by the teaching of Christ. But such codes and standards have been worked out with his fellow workers and not with his fellow Christians. He is aware that in the development of industry, in its labor union as well as in its managerial sides, the church has up till now played little or no part, and he is often irritated now by the desire of the church to intrude.

The man of whom we are thinking is a member of the church. He wants to live as a Christian and he takes this to mean that he must demonstrate his Christian obedience in his life with his family, in the way he treats his neighbors, in his leisure-time activities, in his social contacts, and in his participation in the worship and life of the church. And here the minister is of peculiar significance. In the area of family life and social contacts and service in the neighborhood the minister can be regarded as a specialist—and therefore as an example. The church member sees the minister as one who honestly tries to live as he preaches and who is not cumbered by the frustration of involvement in activities where his creed cannot run. He is a citizen and probably a parent. He has had the privilege of studying the meaning of the faith in relation to domestic and social life. It is in these areas that he is able and expected to speak with authority — and experience.

So the minister becomes the model for the member of the church. The piety of the laity is based on the piety of the clergy. And the more sincere and humble the parson is, the firmer is the hold of his example on his people — and therefore the more dangerous. For the minister cannot follow the layman into the strains, the responsibilities, and the temptations that belong to his industrial life. The example of the minister does not help him in these. So if he feels a call to a deeper obedience in Christ's service, he is not likely to feel that his duty is to face the problem of a Christian in the uncharted area of his industrial life. He is much more likely to follow the minister into the area of the minister's job. He sees his Christian life in terms of his family and social life and assumes that fuller obedience implies full-time service in this area. So he thinks he should become a minister or at least give all the time he can to assisting the work of the minister.

This imitation of the minister is sincere and in many ways inevitable, but it is disastrous for the development of the lay life and witness of the church. It has imposed on the church a ministerial form of piety which the laity has never known before.

It is the ministerial domination of congregational life and the imposition of the ministerial image upon the laity that have clericalized the church in the West in a way unknown before this century. The taking of the minister as the standard for the layman is one of the reasons for the decline of participation by members of the church in responsible political action. There is no doubt that many of those engaged in political life are sincere and active members of the church. There are more such men than we sometimes think. We cannot dismiss their connection with the church by saying that a church affiliation is an asset in appealing for votes. But there is a greater gulf than before between church life and political life. The leaders of the local church are not often the leaders in local political life as was the case last century.

Today the layman, especially the more religious layman, thinks it better for him not to meddle with politics. He finds his justification in that the minister tends not to get involved in politics. This attitude of the minister is understandable, if mistaken. He does not wish to identify himself with controversy. He does not wish to identify himself with one section of his people. He may tell his people that it is their duty to take politics responsibly, to join a political party and not to be afraid of their opinions. But his example is more effective than his words. The cost of his example is not the loss that society suffers from the lack of his political contribution but in the loss to political life of the mass of the members of the church who have decided that the higher Christian obedience is to follow the example of the minister and avoid the mess of politics. Where an example calls for inactivity and can appeal to the so-called virtue of impartiality it is generally followed. Detachment from political action has come to be regarded as a Christian virtue. This has been disastrous for the country — and for the church.

Earlier in this chapter we said that this minister-centered conception of the congregation grew up without anyone's planning it and certainly without any nefarious scheming on the part of the minister. Most clergy want to see their people develop initiative and responsibility. Most of the laity would repudiate any desire to become "little ministers." The institution as it has developed has forced them into this position and — what is as important — has affected the relationship of clergy and laity in a dangerous way. It has put the parson in a position of dominance inside the congregation and set him on a pedestal of example unknown before. Often the parson is acutely uncomfortable in this position in which he finds himself. He would rather be doing other things. He may find relief in preaching another way from the pulpit. But he is held in this position by the people on whom the congregation most depends for its continuing life, who feel that this life depends on his being in that position. He is often irritated by them. And because of his position he is uneasy with those others whom he would like to see as the active laymen of the church, but who for all their liking for the minister personally, can find no sense in this minister-centered church. And the laymen are uncomfortable, even those who are quite happy with this pattern of church life. They have lost the independence and the zest that their forefathers knew. The layman has become the shadow of the minister. He knows that he should be doing something else, something of his own. But he does not know what it is and no one will tell him.

The relationship of minister and layman has become half industrial and half pastoral. The minister is the boss who knows the rules and holds the authority. He is also the pastor of the flock. Each relationship implies superiority. The combination is uncomfortable for both sides.

Somehow the layman has to break out from this imprisoning pattern. Somehow the church has to find a new way of life. The layman has to find what is his own peculiar task in the world. He has to find the form of his own vocation in the church as well as the meaning of vocation in his work in the world. The clergy can and must help in this. How they will do so is their peculiar problem. How the layman finds heart to revolt is another matter.

The layman has to find his task — in his daily job, in his neighborhood, in his nation, and in the church. To this we turn in the next four chapters.

4. *The Layman at Work*

The church has at long length begun to understand the importance of *work* to most lay people — the amount of time they spend on the job, the amount of energy it takes, the amount of ambition and forward planning and castle-building in the executive clouds which some people achieve — and the utter lack of any hopes for promotion in the future which is what so many people have so early to accept. It is necessary to stress that work is not *all* that lay people do — for some well-meaning Christian leaders seem almost to forget that most men and women have both leisure time and holidays — which they may well put more energy into than their work demands, and which (if the economists are to be trusted) will more and more become their major interests. It is ironic to reflect that the church is just beginning to be interested in industrial chaplains, and labor unions, and a theology of hard work, when the industrial revolution is moving on inexorably to a time when perhaps there will be only a minority of planners and executives who will find their chief interests in their paid working hours.

Nevertheless, we are not all living in Southern California, nor are we New York electrical workers with a thirty-hour week. For a long time yet, many British and American people (let alone most Africans and Asiatics) will be glad enough to work forty hours a week or longer, since they cannot achieve a decent standard of living for themselves or their families without doing so. Let us stress their *families:* one of the most impressive facets of industrial life in modern society is the way in which men gladly undertake long hours of overtime in order to equip their homes with consumer durables, or keep their children at school, in a way which they would have thought incredible before the 1939 war. Dr. Ferdinand Zweig has shown us in *The Worker in an Affluent Society* the extraordinary standards of domestic loyalty and self-sacrifice to be found in very many British working-class homes — and practical experience in Glasgow or in Southeast Lancashire will confirm this. Very many ordinary Christian workers have done a fine job since 1945 in making the most of their little homes, giving their wives some decent kitchen equipment, letting the kids stay at school longer — and giving the family (including Grandpa) a great deal of pleasure in Sunday trips away from the dreary surroundings of our industrial slums. It may be suggested that in this way they have shown a fine sense of making the most of that state of life they have had to put up with.

But of course there is more to be said about work than that. The trouble is that Christian writings about work (especially other people's work) are so often hopelessly pious or idealistic. As Dr. J. H. Oldham wrote in *Life Is Commitment:* "Men have to earn their living by their labour, to support their families, to order their life in communities, to carry on the tasks of civilization. It is only a few who can contract out of these activities and these are carried on the shoulders of the rest. Since that is so, the question for the majority of Christians is: How can I serve God in my work — as farmer, producer, manufacturer, technician, scientist, administrator and so on? I often have a feeling of impatience when I read discussions by theologians of the relation of the Christian to the world, because the whole discussion seems to me conducted from a detached point of view, quite different from that of the man actively engaged in the affairs of this life. The latter cannot view the world from outside: he is in the thick of it. The question, to which such men want an answer is what difference being a Christian makes to the things that they do and the decision that they make during the working day and the working week. Why should a scientist or engineer or an administrator attach any great importance to religion unless it says to him: 'In the work you are doing day by day you are a partner of God in his work of creation and the realization of his purpose for the family of the sons of men.' "

It is the great merit of the modern teaching about the Holy Communion that many lay people are now taught to consider their daily work and life sacramentally. Nevertheless, the teaching sermons at such Communions can be hopelessly pious and unrealistic. At their worst, they merit the harsh words of Dr. Truman B. Douglass, who in January, 1961, spoke to the American National Council of Churches on Christ and Technology. He complained, "I think it must be maddening to responsible laymen, when ministers tell them that the complex problems of our society can be solved by narrowly religious methods, by a little more prayer, a little more Bible reading, a little more application of the teachings of Christ." And he added: "Do not misunderstand me. I am in favour of all these activities. But the Bible and the teaching of Christ have very little to tell us specifically about how to improve agricultural productivity in a technically retarded area, or how to attack endemic disease in a nation without a public health programme."

As John Lawrence commented at the Anglican Congress at Toronto in August, 1963, in such matters "it is the parson who is the layman, and he must acknowledge this explicitly before he can gain the confidence of the laity and persuade them that he knows what he means when he talks about the calling of lay people. It is for the clergy to challenge the laity: it is for the laity to find out for themselves how they can meet the challenge."

This chapter must try to avoid these dangers. And the theory of the matter is not obscure. There are five ways in which a man must obey God in his work. In the first place, he must serve his neighbor on the job — his fellow workers, and those immediately above and below him. As Bill Wright, the social and industrial adviser to the Bishop of Durham, wrote in *Item* in June, 1962: "If a man treats other men's sons in different and more degrading ways than he would treat his own, he's had it. . . . If you can never be wrong, never apologize, won't do a thing after finishing time, will only do what's strictly required of you during working hours, have no obvious interest in Trade Union affairs, have no time for new ideas, you're not the person to try convincing young people of anything — least of all the Christian Faith." We are of the firm opinion that this must normally involve joining a union or a professional association — and trying as best he can to squeeze the time to become one of the active minority in that union or association.

In the second place he must serve his customer — directly if he makes personal contact with him, and indirectly if he designs, or grows, or assembles, or paints, or packs articles which eventually a customer will buy. This may be thought rather an old-fashioned point to make, and we are certainly not suggesting the naïve Victorian middle-class axiom, "The customer is always right." But the customer is one of our "neighbors," and has his rights; *and we are all customers of one another in a modern industrial economy.* Thirdly, he must serve the firm or public authority he works for — and the shareholders if there are any. Fourthly, he must serve the community in which he works and lives and sleeps in safety. And fifthly, he must serve his "calling" — he must respect and try to add to the knowledge and learning and skill and traditional know-how in his particular job. This is true for motor mechanics, for accountants, for lawyers, for airline clerks, just as much as for old-style "craftsmen"; and it is fascinating to reflect on the different ethical and educational skills which have in the last fifty years developed, for example, in market research, in airport management, in television repairs, or in telephone engineering.

Even the most routine mass-production worker (where it is especially important for Christians to avoid idealistic guff) *has* an obligation to work reliably, though maybe with little joyous enthusiasm. As Tom Chapman wrote in *Christian Comment* in January, 1963: "His service to the community is real. His contribution to the end-product is to do precisely what he is told to do by someone in authority. This makes one small part in the jig-saw, the end of which he rarely ever sees. The customer who buys it, he almost never meets."

All these five ways in which a layman must "serve" in his daily work are not at all only for well-educated people with higher education. It is worth emphasizing this point again: we are not interested in any theories for the working laity that only apply to university graduates. The ordinary layman has to work all this out in the concrete details of his Monday-morning life, even if he cannot articulate clear theories about them. It is depressing to reflect that the word "service" has now been degraded by commercial advertising just when the concept of serving your neighbor at work (even when you don't know him) has become of such tremendous importance in our modern interdependent society. For instance, it is commonplace for economists to point out the increasing importance in an affluent society of the "service trades." The ordinary production of automobiles and telephones is increasingly achieved by fewer and fewer workers who with automated machinery nevertheless produce more and more at lower and lower cost. We find as a result that we are better and better off, and increasingly we spend our greater incomes on vacations or entertainment, on meals out or on insurance. These service trades therefore employ more and more workers, whose attitude to work and to us as customers is of the first importance if we are to enjoy our travels, our meals out—or even our contacts with the insurance man.

Yet in Britain so many people have gone sour about personal service jobs. No doubt, in the past, very many middle-class people imposed upon the lower orders; but there seems sometimes to be a mass conspiracy in English cafés that to be inefficient is to be independent, and to be courteous is to be servile.

Very many industrial leaders find themselves just as puzzled about this matter of "serving one another" as church leaders are. Indeed, under conditions of full employment (which try their capacities for real leadership to breaking point) they sometimes talk hopefully about the "good influence" which industrial chaplains may have, and wistfully about the sober and docile types which the little chapels used to produce.

To put things bluntly, if you treat men as peasants, you will get what you deserve; and it must be admitted that this sometimes goes for Christian employers too, particularly those in charge of small old-fashioned plants. It was amusing to notice the reactions of some jute employers in Dundee when the National Cash Register Company of the U.S.A. started bringing enlightened personnel methods into the city. There are still some small factories in Lancashire and Yorkshire where the men queue up in the rain for their pay—and a girl in the warm office inside (who is "staff" and therefore privileged) sees nothing unchristian in keeping them waiting. There are still schools where seniority or university degrees among the staff, and academic ability or social background among the pupils counts for too much; and where a Christian principal rarely recognizes the cleaners as fellow workers with him in the school by asking them in to school services and functions. And, let it be said, there are church "leaders" and bureaucrats who sometimes forget that the welfare of the frontline troops is the first concern of their officers at the end of a hard battle. There is only one rule for personal contacts, "To love your neighbor as yourself"; but not many of the social habits of our time help us to remember this.

All this implies that Christians who are fortunate or unfortunate enough to find themselves in "top" positions have additional Christian responsibilities. Many of our churches are predominantly middle-class: this has many serious consequences, but it does mean that we have a strong representation among the managerial and professional occupations. It can be accepted that many Christian managers are anxious to behave decently with their subordinates (and even with the most awkward labor union representatives). It is not clear whether they have always been challenged to consider critically their attitudes to their *customers,* and whether they ought so easily to accept the traditional trade customs of price-fixing and so on. It is even less certain that many of them have ever, since they left college, considered their duty to their "craft," to the specialized skill that gives them their responsible positions and, no doubt, comfortable houses and cars as well. The important pioneer lay center at Hartford, Connecticut, has held a series of discussions with professional engineers; and many of these men have admitted that they feel guilty about the way in which their expert knowledge has been prostituted by the salespeople or the "designers" in their firms. They have been ordered not to produce a first-class or even a good solid job, but instead something gimmicky and flashy which will fit the fashion in consumer durables for the time being—and then wear out quickly enough to provide a replacement market. Of course it is impossible to make every car like a Rolls-Royce, and there is a fair compromise to be made between quality and price—it is not necessarily immoral to design a cheap article for Woolworth's. But the point they make in their reports is one that Christians have evaded too often.

Another deeply ethical problem in modern industry has been expressed recently by some discussions of the Iona Community's industrial committee. Modern production techniques are increasingly automatic, not merely with regard to the machinery involved but in the rigid and inflexible demands that they make on the people in the plant — at all levels of production from the fitter to quite senior professional engineers. The dangers of this can be exaggerated (and Christians have been much too sentimental about the joys of "craft" production in the past); but even the most realistic corporation executive, who knows that not only his firm's profits but our whole standard of living depends on such production techniques, is sometimes driven to ask, "What are we *doing* to these men we employ?" It may be part of an answer to these fears to say that, after all, men will spend less and less of their time in such production — but it may also be something of an evasion of the question.

The important thing is for a Christian to learn to *think* about his job in a Christian way. Maybe he has to admit that it is nothing very creative, that it's just a way of getting a living. Maybe he can see exciting possibilities in it — or maybe he is lucky enough and young enough to make another choice. But the important thing is to realize what you are doing between breakfast and the evening meal. And there are enormous obstacles to such clear self-assessment.

Young executives and managers, in particular, have to cut their way through the jungle of modern assumptions about the "rat race." This is a popular enough thing to debunk at Christian conferences or in sociological novels: we have to ask how a young graduate from Manchester or M.I.T. *could* contract out of it, and also whether he should. Both in the United States, and certainly in Britain, there are plenty of firms and government departments where promotion is normally sought and granted in perfectly honorable ways, and where any attempt at character assassination of your rivals or sharp bargaining to gain a contract is the surest way to be damned forever by your superiors. Christians ought indeed to examine with more care how such an ethical climate is produced in firm "A" when it is conspicuously lacking in firm "B," and indeed sometimes in industry "X" when it is not there in industry "Y." The residual influence of nineteenth-century business morality and of the famous British "public school" code of behavior deserve our critical attention, not our sneers.

On the other hand, our educational systems for "top" people does make it difficult for many of its products to treat other people as genuine human beings, and not as "peasants." Undoubtedly graduates from the more famous colleges in Britain and the States often operate an informal network of privilege, which means the proper equality of opportunity for higher jobs is openly or subtly denied. There can also develop an "antiestablishment" prejudice, particularly among labor union organizers, which equally poisons human relations in a factory or industry. We have known some discussions among Christian workers which forgot that even a capitalist boss may be your "neighbor" and deserves a fair hearing.

All these complications and qualifications about relating our Christian faith to daily work have undoubtedly meant that in the last two hundred years very many Christians have evaded the issue. They have been good family Christians, good neighborhood Christians, and even good Sunday church Christians. But they have felt unable to take their faith with them on the seven fifteen bus to their plants, or the eight ten train to town, or the nine thirty Cadillac to the board meeting. It is always possible, of course, that this is simply a failure of moral courage: we are not as a church very good at producing moral heroes, and a touch of scrupulosity or Salvation Army doggedness may, more often than we suspect, be the simple remedy to our ineffectiveness. But this is a rather easy comment to make, and sometimes very unfair.

A great number of men feel that they cannot honestly be a "proper Christian" at work and keep their jobs. They must keep their jobs—if only for the sake of their wives and families. So they assume that they just can't be "proper" Christians; and since hypocrisy is, thank God, one of the most disliked attitudes among men today, they feel it much better not to pretend to be particularly Christian about their daily work. They would rather just be considered "decent types," and leave it at that. To be a "Christian," a "religious type," would mean either becoming a hopelessly pious Bible-thumper or pretending to some kind of 100 percent perfectionism *which they know they can't achieve* as salesmen, as bus drivers, or even as schoolteachers.

Here is the crux of the matter. Very many men and women in jobs won't consciously relate their faith to their jobs because they don't feel they're "good enough." This is a quite damnable and false idea of Christian perfectionism. A Christian is not a 100 percent perfect human being, he is a sinner saved by the grace of God. Of course there ought to be some fruits of the Spirit evident in his daily life, of course he ought to keep himself free of scandalous behavior either on the job or off it, but he can't achieve perfection, as most men understand it. And he is not being pious or hypocritical if he tries to relate his loyalty to his Lord to his daily work: he is simply doing his plain duty. If he refused to do this even out of some wrong sense of inadequacy or humility, he would be neglecting his plain duty. His sins of omission in trying to run his work and his religion in two separate compartments would be much more serious than anything else. Maybe he will make a mess of things, maybe sometimes he will let down his Lord by not protesting about some abuse or racket, maybe sometimes he will make a fool of himself and his church by protesting too much—but none of this will matter compared with the fact that he is at least struggling, with God's help, to live a consistent Christian life.

It was excellent to see that this point was a main feature of the Laity meetings of the World Council of Churches Assembly at New Delhi in November, 1961. Mr. E. V. Matthews, an Indian lawyer, put the plain question: "What do I do about doubtful practices in my profession in my country? Do I join with them? How dirty are we lay people in the world to get our hands?" And Miss Mollie Batten, principal of William Temple College, in Rugby, said this as part of her reply: "Rarely will the choice be between good and evil. It will be a decision between alternatives, both of which are partly good and partly evil." And she added: "In so far as it is for the layman to make a decision and to act upon it, insofar as they make mistakes . . . God will accept their recognition of this, forgive them and give them power to try again. This is our faith."

She also remarked: "There will be many occasions on which the layman has to make up his mind whether, in the particular circumstances with which he is confronted, the time has come to make the crucial stand, or to wait and fight another day. I think we have to learn from Jesus Christ that there are many occasions on which the right thing to do is to wait, in order to remain in the situation. When the final stand has to be made, then we must remember that we are called to witness to the greatest power structure in the world, the kingdom of God. 'The light shines on in the dark, and the darkness has never quenched it.'" (John 1:5, NEB.)

In brief: the Christian in his daily life has to learn the art of *responsible compromise* (a word that needs to be rescued from its derogatory connotations). Sometimes, of course, he must openly protest, offer his resignation, risk his own and even his family's prosperity. Sometimes — but not always, and not as often as the outsiders suggest, whether they be clerical or lay. Of course, talk about "responsible compromise" may very easily slide into irresponsible compromise; and there are plenty of subtle temptations to fall in with doubtful but profitable commercial practices which Christians simply ought to avoid. It is fair to say that a Christian ought never to compromise with an easy conscience — that he ought always to watch what he is doing, to be *uneasy* about a decline in business standards, to remind himself that God may call him to make a fool of himself in the eyes of the world. Yet it would be a poor thing if, for instance, all Christians in West Africa avoided the legal profession because of their scruples, or if all church people avoided city government contracts in the States or city police work in Britain.

Each personal crisis demands a different prayerful solution. God may ask one man to resign and another to comply, and neither will be completely happy about his actions. Think of the moral dilemmas of Christians in government service under the Nazis, or in certain countries today. But what is clear is that both those who stay and those who resign may be doing what they conscientiously believe to be right — and outsiders must at all costs resist the easy moral judgment, particularly in condemning those who do *not* contract out of public or business life.

Penry Jones, writing about his work for television in the March, 1963, *Christian Comment,* gave an excellent example of the kind of job that Christians must not be afraid to undertake. He wrote: "The religious TV producer is a man of divided loyalties. He is responsible both to the churches and to the world of television. . . . He stands in the Church, but he must at the same time have enough imagination, sympathy and respect to stand for the nonchurchman. This is his frontier, and he betrays his trust rather than serves it if he sacrifices too much to the wishes and opinions of his masters — be they in television or be they in the churches."

Men at the top have a greater freedom, for they can

generally survive if they do offer to resign. Yet their very position at the top makes for a continual confusion of ethical priorities, and the pace of decision and the pressure of competition from business or professional rivals (known in the most socialist countries) make calm self-assessment very difficult. Men at the bottom — or part of the way up — have less economic freedom, for their families must eat; and they have also a real duty to try to reach the top, where their chances of influencing their chosen profession or occupation will be so much greater. Yet there comes a time when even the most rosy possibilities of advancement and influence later cannot quite condone the shabby trick that is expected now. And yet — what is the sense of getting a reputation as an awkward so-and-so?

W. E. Gladstone faced such dilemmas in his youth. In the first place, he only reluctantly and slowly decided on a career as a politician, instead of entering Holy Orders. And then in the early years he was always examining his conscience on matters of government policy, sometimes, it seems to us, overscrupulously — but sometimes asking the blunt moral question that almost every politician around him was evading. Lord Palmerston, for many years his prime minister, had to put up with a good deal; he is said to have remarked: "That young man is always coming round with his resignation in his pocket." But Mr. Gladstone survived, somehow, and survived as a politician. He was four times prime minister of England; and in the end, even his bitterest political enemies recognized his moral qualities. He was a Christian politician, which is sometimes more than being a Christian bishop.

Clearly, a life of responsible (as distinct from unconscious) compromise is a dangerous one. But here, perhaps, is some of the zest of the Christian life which we have lost with our safe platitudes and pietism. Certainly, it is of the first importance that young people should sometimes pick the ethically tough jobs, and feel that this is their Christian duty. If only the institutional church would recognize this, and find ways to support the young politician, or shopkeeper, or assembly supervisor, instead of wishing all the time that he would go into what are (quite erroneously) considered the ethically "pure" jobs of teaching or the ministry. (For teachers and ministers, quietly and rather shamefacedly, spend a great deal of their time too "compromising" — we hope responsibly.)

It is very easy to say that men and women must make responsible compromises prayerfully, that they must wrestle with their problems on their knees before the Lord, and that then it will all become clear. Sometimes it will (but probably after a fair ration of wrestling, a good deal more than Jacob's night or so). *Sometimes it will not* — despite all that the pietists can say about divine guidance or answers to prayer. In the last twenty years, there have been a good many Christians in "gray" jobs, in the Armed Services, for instance, or in the resistance movement in Germany, or in the revolution in Communist China, or in the mental hospitals, who have not seen the perfect answer, and who have indeed known that the "grays" are part of the very texture of modern life. God is gracious enough to give to his servants some assurance that they can persevere through the fogs of life: but the fogs do not always disperse after a few hours. It is this kind of reality which the church should teach us to face, and it is this kind of life which we should be taught to pray about and to relate to the Sacraments.

5. The Layman and the Modern World

The London *Church Times* in November, 1962, had an important editorial on the need for a Christian voice to be heard in social and political questions. It said: "The easy way is the wrong way. The tempting answer is for the Church as an organized body (i.e., through its Assembly, the Convocations and the like) to hold debates and pass resolutions on the topics in question. This habit, which now extends with tiresome regularity to such wider bodies as the British Council of Churches and the World Council of Churches, has almost nothing to recommend it. For one thing, the debate takes place long after the event concerned. And the passing of resolutions deceives people into thinking that they have achieved something, whereas in fact they have not made the slightest difference to the problem involved. It is a sound general rule that bodies should confine themselves to those fields where they have some actual power to affect the situation."

Harsh words. And this editorial rather underestimates the educational value of these church discussions. They don't affect the world outside, but they do make the people in the Assembly or committee involved more alive to the problems under discussion. But we would heartily agree with the editor of the *Church Times* when he goes on: "It is through the political parties and Parliament, through the organs of local government at every level, that Christians must speak and act and seek to influence events for good. Their contribution can be just as specifically christian as if it were attempted through an ecclesiastical body. The difference is, that it may also be effective."

The trouble is that when we consider the complex problems of national and international affairs, and try to formulate more than pious platitudes about them, we are very tempted to assume that only Christians with expert knowledge or high general education can comment constructively on them. So many attempts to popularize these problems and to suggest brief and palatable solutions to them are trivial and superficial: so many well-meaning little Christian pamphlets on, for example, the H-bomb or urban renewal fall between two stools — they are not scholarly enough to impress the secular specialist, nor are they readable enough to attract the attention of the man in the street.

We are completely convinced that it is the duty of *every* Christian to take the responsibility for political decisions, and not to shirk the effort — maybe the chore — of keeping himself informed about both local and national politics. It may well be that some national and international problems require high expert knowledge and experience, and in that case it is for all of us to take the trouble to learn what such experts have to tell us. (The sheer quantity of such information now available through television and the paperbacks is most impressive.) But we cannot, in any kind of liberal democracy, simply shrug our shoulders and say, "Let's leave it to the people who *know*." And very often ordinary church members with or without much academic education will have valuable local experience to contribute to the matter in hand. A shop-floor worker, a working-class housewife down the street, a member of the Teamsters' Union — all these have something valuable to say about Puerto Ricans in Manhattan or Jamaicans in Birmingham, England, and the church should be careful to listen to them. And let us all remember that it is the people like this who have much to contribute to a practical solution of living together with new immigrants, and that if we attempt any theoretical solutions in our church discussion groups without listening to them, we shall soon become irrelevant. More than this, it is an essential part of every Christian's daily duty to consider, to some extent and in some practical down-to-earth ways, his obligations to a world on which he depends for his own and his family's prosperity. Our "neighbors" to whom we owe our Christian love are difficult to define nowadays, but they certainly include some people outside our hometown, and overseas; our responsibilities to them ought to take up a portion of every Christian's time.

As Dr. George MacLeod insists in *Only One Way Left:* "Political concern should grow inevitably from the very nature of the Gospel preached and the Bible interpreted. . . . In industrial parishes the state of housing, the lack of playing fields, the economic plight of pensioners, Sunday work . . . all lead us into political issues. It is important not to pass them by as things incidental, as if the spiritual were our department, comparable to the insurance man, the gas meter man, the health visitor, the instalment collector and the rent raiser in their departments. So to pass by is merely to perpetuate the non-Biblical view of religion already too present in the mind of our people."

Of course ordinary church people will work this out in practical ways and with reference to local activities. Sometimes this can be a small part in a national effort like Christian Aid Week for refugees — a notable achievement of the British Council of Churches, which has done more than thousands of wordy documents to tell Britain that the churches are capable of working together. Often the man in the street's Christian concerns must be expressed in local and in national elections — Miss Janet Lacey, the famous director of Christian Aid, herself wrote in *Christian Comment* for April, 1963: "The world-wide physical problems of hunger can only be resolved by political and United Nations action. What we must do as individuals is to throw sentimentality overboard and face the fact that austerity lunches and dipping our hands irresponsibly into our pockets as a response to mass appeals are *not* deep sacrifices; and they do not do much to help us understand the human problem of the hungry person, and the way people live in the other half of the world. They are social occasions and they help to raise money, but we should not delude ourselves by thinking they are getting to the heart of the matter."

And Canon Max Warren, formerly General Secretary of the English Church Missionary Society, demanded of his fellow Anglicans at Toronto in 1963 "a much more serious attempt to understand and grapple with the economic issues of our world." He pointed out the value of the Institute of Strategic Studies in London (which was largely started by a group of Christian laymen) and added: "Is there anywhere a comparable 'Institute of Economic Studies' in which some of the implications of the population explosion are being studied by Christian men, who are concerned with the ethical implications of economic policies? Such an Institute would be quite invaluable not only to enable Christians to be intelligently informed about economic problems, and thus to take an intelligent part in forming a responsible public opinion. It would, I believe, be of immense value, incidentally, in affording guidance to the Church."

In the same way, Christian leaders are at long last realizing the importance of local government organizations. City and county administrations are often the Cinderellas of our public life, and yet their budgets of millions of dollars a year affect very deeply our welfare and our attitude toward the underprivileged.

What is needed now is not so much generalized exhortations to vote more often at local elections, but a thorough examination of the structure of political power at local and county level, and a drastic and at the same time sympathetic appraisal of the moral opportunities and temptations that face local officials. It is depressing to think of the number of local officials in Britain to whom "the church" means no more than the Church of England (or perhaps the Church of Rome) being "difficult" about church schools. The Rt. Rev. E. R. Wickham, Bishop of Middleton, has started a most interesting series of informal discussions with local leaders in Southeast Lancashire, and other Christians have made great impact in local life in towns like Leeds and Glasgow. Yet too often they have been regarded as individuals who took this up as their "hobby" (and might it not have been more profitable to serve on the Ex-Prisoners' Association or the Christian Grandmothers' Society?). They have been the forgotten representatives of Christ and his church, trailing night after night to the rather dreary discussions of local councils and party caucuses.

Other ordinary Christians can do great good by *sensible* criticism of local schools, hospitals, and housing. Many British people have been too patient about local deficiencies in our welfare state, perhaps particularly in the north of England. There is all the difference in the world between petulant nagging of local authorities and nurses and teachers, and a well-mannered insistence on our own and particularly our *neighbor's* rights. There is nothing particularly Christian in submitting to the kind of hospital which implies that ordinary patients are lucky to get any attention at all, at any time. There is a whole technique of courteous Christian agitation to be worked out — which will be neither fussing, nor petty bullying of local officials (which will merely make them retreat into a hard official shell of *their* "rights"), nor yet just a pulling of strings for ourselves or our children."

Not all our social concerns have to be worked out in government offices, national or local. For instance, both in the United States and in Britain, there is a wide gap between the "legal" rights of Jews or Negroes and their acceptance as first-class citizens. Much must be done by legal process and administrative action: more still by personal friendliness and informal discussion over a cup of coffee. How many middle-class Christians have ever joined, even if halfheartedly, in anti-Jewish gossip, and attempts to keep them out of local golf clubs? How many Christians accept, almost without ever thinking out what a *sinful* thing it is, stereotyped sneers and gossip about Negroes or Russians? How many Christian parents cause their children to stumble by encouraging such attitudes from an early age? And how many deliberately attempt to teach their children that in Christ we are one family — and that, for instance, for every rowdy and unpleasant person of another race you can find another with admirably thrifty and clean habits.

Of course Christians who by birth, education, or sheer native ability penetrate to the "governing class" today have special responsibilities in national life. Some of their peculiar opportunities and temptations have been admirably discussed in a recent book, *Equality and Excellence,* written by Daniel Jenkins for the Christian Frontier Council. Such people are often very busy indeed, and they tend to remark with justified irritation: "How on earth am I to find time to keep informed about underground H-bomb tests, the ratio of road deaths to the speed of passenger cars, the economic problems of Fiji, the psychological influences of TV and so on? I know enough to know I don't know enough to say anything really authoritative on all these things: it's better (and more honest) for me to keep my mouth shut — and leave it to the bishops to expose their ignorance with 'Christian' statements of one kind and another."

Let us concede at once that such people have a point. They cannot take an intelligent and informed Christian interest in everything, not even in everything mentioned in the serious Sunday papers. We ought always to respect a man who says honestly, "I really don't know anything much about X, though I do know that it's more complicated than it looks." Nevertheless it is possible for a well-educated Christian to make himself very well informed about *one or two* issues of the day, and moderately well informed about a number of others — and this is his plain duty. It is depressing to think of the number of Christian graduates who lose the art of "working up" a report on an important question — unless their boss at work suddenly demands a memo on it. We would dare to suggest that a number of young graduate mothers might serve the church very well by reading up on a subject like Cuba or Eastern Germany — even if their domestic ties mean that it is only their family and relations and immediate neighbors who benefit from their reading. It is even true that such overburdened wives (like their overburdened executive husbands) will gain mentally and psychologically by trying to master one or two subjects completely unrelated to their daily chores. And the church of Christ will gain tremendously; for in a few years instead of dull bridge-playing couples there can be people able to speak with some authority on their chosen topics. And there are a good many subjects on which the Christian who has read a dozen books can help far more than the man or woman who has only glanced at the *Reader's Digest* article on the subject. After a year or two, the whole local church, including the ministers, would be glad to sit at his or her feet.

The position of Christian young people is of great importance here. Many of our churches are largely middle class, and our universities have a large percentage of church or ex-church members. It is infuriating to contemplate how, with certain honorable exceptions, these young people have never been taught to consider their national and international responsibilities in the light of their Christian faith. Many of them are frankly apathetic about public affairs, others are privately worried but reluctant to commit themselves to responsible or irresponsible public action; most of them have associated their churches with a purely private morality and pleasant social activities.

It must be admitted that Christian teachers, both in Sunday schools and much more in the day schools, have a special importance in all this. Christian teachers often join with their colleagues in being either far too utopian or far too casual about national and international affairs. (Perhaps women teachers are sharply different from men teachers here?) A good many teachers who are loyal members of their local churches are content to take — and to pass on to their pupils — opinions from the less responsible daily papers or from some trivial TV quiz. They are as likely as any other middle-class professional people to reflect the views of the outer suburbs — and yet surely they have a special duty to think more objectively about class and race and status-seeking. Sociologists in both Britain and the United States have given some devastating examples of the way our education systems can work against working-class children from less privileged homes. What every Christian teacher must do is ask himself: "Could this apply to our school? Have I, even without noticing it, favored the nice children, dismissed some of the others as 'They only come from X street,' contributed my damnable mite to the weight of class and race prejudice in my country today?"

The very "top" people in Western countries often include confessing Christians — for instance, in politics we need only mention Dr. Adenauer, Mr. Macmillan, and the late President Kennedy. It is the clear duty of ordinary Christian people to pray regularly for them — as well as criticizing them when we must. Those who know them, and the senior civil servants and industrialists and technologists and journalists who help them, have a very special duty to support them prayerfully and intelligently. Christians are sometimes where real power is — or at least very near it — and it seems that they in particular feel the loneliness and the moral responsibilities of their position. It may be remarked that some church leaders in London and Washington and such places, fulfill a real function of the whole body of Christ in supporting them in their daily lives.

6. The Layman and His Neighbors

A man lives his life with others. His society makes him what he is. But today a man's job comes first. His work decides where he lives and how he lives. This is why we have thought of a man and his job — and of his place in nation and world — before we think of him in his neighborhood. His job usually decides who his neighbors are.

This is a change in the country's life. In earlier days, and not so long ago, it was his neighborhood that determined a man's job, or, at least, kept the choice between the narrow limits of what his locality offered. In many cases there was not much chance of his moving elsewhere or of his finding work if he did. Often all a man could do was to follow his father's occupation and in many cases, as for instance in the coal mines of Scotland till the seventeenth century, he was bound to do so. Nowadays we think of a hereditary job as a mark of privilege; and perhaps question the efficiency of a system by which a youth inherits directorships or a family business or land. We forget that for most men in the world today, and for some in this country not so long ago, hereditary occupation can be near slavery.

Today, even if there is not so much choice for young people as we would wish, our attitude toward work and neighborhood has radically changed. We take it for granted that a man's job may set him on the move and send him far from home. Home for many is not the place where they work — but the place to which they return for holidays or for retirement. Men, of course, have always been on the move in search of food. In the past, economic necessity sent men from home in search of work. The clearances in the

Highlands of Scotland sent men by the thousands to Canada. The potato famine in Ireland sent thousands to the United States. Famine and unemployment sent men on the move in the past and send men on the move today. Men know that work is what they must have to live and to support their families, and they go where there is the hope of finding it.

Today work comes first for almost all. It is today not only the economically underprivileged who is on the move in search of work, who has to go where work is or where he thinks it is. Those who are so privileged that they have a choice of jobs are equally on the move. The higher they have risen on the ladder of promotion in their occupation, the more likely they are to have moved and to be still moving. Success as well as need sets men on the move. The student population is likewise on the move, having to seek a place to study before finding a place to live, and, in increasing numbers, leaving home to do so.

So our population becomes more fluid and will become even more so.

This is a very different situation from the one our grandparents knew and which is reflected in so much of the literature of the last century. Then a man often — even in the States — grew up in the village or town in which he was born and in which he had his family roots. He knew his neighbors from childhood, their children were his playmates, he married one who had shared this life, and, as he grew older, he became even more personally entangled in the complex relationships of a closely related society. In such a community, to go to London or New York was an adventure and the arrival of a stranger an event. In such a society a man's job did not matter so much as his place in the community. His place in the community gave him his status and his security.

Today things are turned the other way around. A man knows his job but does not know his neighbor. His job is the stable thing in his life — the thing that gives him security and status, the thing he must keep. His neighborhood is always changing. He does not expect to find any permanence there.

When today we think of a man's neighborhood we must think of something quite different from the definite geographical area of close relationships of family, work, and sport which was a man's neighborhood fifty years ago. His family will not today necessarily live close around him. He may travel far from his home to go to his work. For his sport and entertainment he may go a great distance by bus or car. The things he talks about are not only the gossip of his immediate neighborhood but many things of a wider interest brought to his attention by radio, television, and the national press. A man's neighborhood has ceased to be a geographical area around which a line could be drawn. It is rather the total of relationships that a man chooses to recognize — all that part of life with which he is consciously in touch.

It includes all those with whom he comes in contact — those with whom he works, those with whom he travels on the bus, those he meets playing or watching games; all the casual contacts that his work and his way of life bring. Some are of his own choosing. Most are accidental and quite arbitrary. Some he may refuse to recognize, but all are his inescapable neighbors. George Macdonald said, "The neighbour is just the man who is next you at the moment, the man with whom any business has brought you in contact." They form an indefinable company stretching out as far as a man's interests and the accidental contacts of his work.

In this sense a man makes his own neighborhood — or at least, chooses it. His job determines the field of his contacts. He himself chooses how many of his countless neighbors he will recognize and determines what his relationship to them will be. He has not the comfort of feeling that his neighbors are given to him, of knowing where he belongs. Instead he has to bear the burden of creating his own neighborhood.

We are often tempted to look back with longing to the settled life of society before the days of modern industry. In particular in the church we tend to think that that pattern of peasant life is the proper setting for the Christian life: that the rural parish of the last century and those before is the social pattern in which the life of the church is most adequately expressed; that, indeed, modern industrial life, with its breakdown of the old village family life and the increasing mobility that it demands of people, is the greatest obstacle of the Christian faith and that our duty is to do all that we can to preserve the old pattern — parish system, family life, and all. We have taken stability and conservatism as the prerequisites of the Christian life.

Dr. John Casteel, of Union Theological Seminary, New York, discussing whether church members in the States should refuse to move at the behest of their employers, has this to say: "Putting aside the question whether such approaches to mobility may not be motivated by a concern to preserve churches as established institutions in stable communities, there is still the impression that these attitudes are based upon the assumption that, somehow, a static pattern of residence is preferable to one of great transiency. Deleterious effects of mobility upon home-life, children, marriages, communities, and other aspects of society, are cited to show how injurious such transiency can be. But to what extent do these consequences come from the fact that our ways of organizing and maintaining home-life, child-nurture, congregations, and the like, are bent to the purpose of preserving a static pattern of living? Suppose our energies were devoted, rather, to preparing people, of all ages and circumstances, not only to survive the strains of mobility, but to use these as opportunities for growth and enrichment of human experience? We have only to recall how destructive of human personality unrelieved fixity of residence, occupation, and environment can be, to give new pertinence to this question."

When we look back to the origins of the church we certainly do not find the stable society we tend to wish for. We find little to support our conventional picture in the actions and teaching of Jesus. The life he chose to live and made his disciples live was more like the unsettled life of men today than was the settled life of a rural parish in the nineteenth century. And it was different from the conventional life of the people of his own time. Jesus himself left the settled life of Nazareth. He told his disciples to leave their homes and their jobs. The work he did and the work on which he sent his men out made them wanderers, with no place to call their own. His teaching challenged the settled life of men, with its clear definition of the claims of family and neighbors. It found its center in the meaning of neighborhood. He gave men a new idea of who their neighbors were and how to treat them. So new was it that men had to ask the question: But who is my neighbor? The accusation against Jesus was that he chose to regard all men and women equally as his neighbors. The accepted teaching of his people and the specific doctrines of the Pharisees stated clearly who were to be regarded as neighbors and excluded all those who did not share their traditions and their way of life. Men were divided into neighbors and strangers. Jesus regarded all men as neighbors. Quite explicitly he included a man's enemies among his neighbors (Matt. 5:43–44). He himself refused no contact, however casual. He gave to his men a new teaching about loving their neighbors. In his own life and in the life of his disciples he substituted for the old comfortable, defined, natural neighborhood the all-inclusive contacts of a rootless life.

The company that Jesus chose to keep was the company of ordinary men. He was more at home with fishermen and farmers, shopkeepers and tax gatherers than with the religious leaders and the priests. His talk was of seedtime and harvest, of buying fields and building houses, of boats and nets. The neighborhood he chose was secular life, the world of ordinary men and women.

This surely is the neighborhood we are discussing when we talk about the tasks of the laity in their neighborhood. Their neighborhood is the ordinary, secular, lay life in which they do their jobs and live their lives and which they share with the other men, women, and children who by choice and accident are their neighbors.

This neighborhood may be difficult to define. Its limits may vary according to a man's interests. He may ignore his obvious neighbors and indeed have little to do with any of them. He may try to cut himself off and live in isolation. But it is his inescapable neighborhood and it belongs to him. He may refuse its demands, but he cannot pass them on to another. Whatever he does or fails to do, he is there in his own right, in his own name. His neighborhood is his own.

His first obligation is to belong to it, to know his natural part in it. This is basic to his being a Christian. Jesus' injunction to us is to love our neighbors as ourselves. It involves our acceptance of all our multitudinous and inescapable neighbors. We can appreciate the love that a man feels for his native countryside or for the city street that was his childhood's home, and how they will appear to him as beautiful and infinitely lovable in his memory. For Jesus, who knew this love, love of neighbor was as unquestioned.

But he had to make this love his new commandment, because it was new and demanding.

A man's neighborhood is given to him and its demands are inescapable. This does not mean that his response is easy or to be taken for granted. The task of a Christian is to widen the conception of neighborhood beyond the bounds that convention sets and to see in the relationships of neighborhood a love that need know no limit. It is in the end to regard no one with whom one has contact, tangible or unseen, as outside his neighborhood.

This is the layman's world. In this world he does his work and lives his life. His work is his own peculiar work and his life is his personal life. But in this life he is never alone. He is a layman, a member of the church. He is expected to be a member of a local congregation. His life as a layman is lived in the fellowship of the church.

So before we discuss in more detail his own peculiar tasks in his neighborhood something should first be said of the task of his church in his neighborhood. For unless his share in the life of his neighborhood is part, and is seen to be part, of the life of the church it will be quite ineffectual as witness and be regarded by others merely as the actions of a well-meaning individual. The local church must manifest the same acceptance of all as neighbors, the same participation in their life as he feels called to in his obedience, if his actions are to be seen as Christian — Christian, that is, not in the vague conventional use of that word but in the sense of expressing the life of Christ.

The layman in his endeavor to find and carry out his task in his neighborhood here comes up against his greatest difficulty. The church, especially in its modern congregational form, has managed to give to those outside the impression of exclusiveness. To them the church often appears as a society of people who think of themselves as different and want to keep themselves distinct. Probably these outsiders don't feel, except in the vaguest way, that the church condemns or criticizes them, as their grandparents would have felt, but this is because they wouldn't bother if the church did criticize. They think of the people who are in the church as a bit different — a bit odd — in their interests, opinions, and actions. Generally they think of them as not doing certain things or not approving of certain things. "You go to church—you won't want to do this." The outside neighbors of the church don't think of the members of the church as having any particular concern with them, except vaguely of trying to get them to go to church.

The attitude of those within the church is different and more important. They are aware that there is a difference between them and those outside. Perhaps they would say that it was their faith but probably, if they were honest with themselves, they would say that the difference was simply that they belonged to the church and the others did not. They would be uncomfortably aware that there ought to be a greater difference in the way they lived. This sense of there being a difference and that this difference lies in their membership of the church makes them feel that they must keep apart, to cultivate this difference. How do we prevent this awareness of difference from becoming a mood that is exclusive and critical of outsiders? Or, to put the question in another way, how can the layman, anxious to obey Jesus' command to love his neighbors, find the support he needs in a church that finds its life in its differences from, and its suspicions of, its nonchurch neighbors?

The church can overcome this false exclusiveness only by returning constantly to the foundation of its faith in Jesus Christ: to the basic doctrine of his incarnation by which we believe that God in Christ identifies himself with all men. We know that he has redeemed the world and that he is Lord of all. It is this faith that unites us to all men. In Christ we know that we are united in love with all men. It is our failure, our weakness, our sin that cuts us off from other men, that makes divisions between men. We often seem to think that it is the other way around: that it is the touch of sinful nature that makes all mankind kin; that it is in our sin that we are united; that it is our faith that cuts us off and makes us different. But it is God who has made us of one blood. It is Christ who has broken down the walls of partition between men. In him all men and all things will find their being, for he has redeemed them. The mission of the church is to declare this and to bear witness to this truth in its life. This doctrine is basic to the recovery of the lay nature of the church. A clericalized church will inevitably stress its difference from other men. A lay church will seek identification in love.

The local church has, therefore, to make this evident in its life and witness in its neighborhood. It must do this if the individual activities of its members are not to be dismissed as the peculiar idiosyncrasies of well-meaning cranks or the peculiar activities of people who are not really representative of the church. So long as the church in the eyes of the people is equated with the activities of the clergy outside the church buildings and the activities of church members inside the church buildings, the change in attitude will have to be seen in what the clergy do outside and in what goes on in church buildings, if the change is to be seen at all.

The work of the clergy is the lesser problem. The minister moves about in his neighborhood. He is seen in the street and in the stores. He has his obvious part in the ordinary affairs of ordinary life. He has to overcome — and generally he wants passionately to overcome — the idea that he is there to serve only his own people in the church. He has to make special efforts to make it be seen that his concern as a clergyman is with the whole range of ordinary activities of his neighborhood.

The estrangement of the world from the church is much more serious than we often think. It is due far more than we think to a *distortion of the teaching of Jesus* which to the outsider is obvious and very strange. The outsider is right in assuming that Jesus belongs to him. The president of the English Methodist Conference, Rev. Leslie Davison, said to them in 1962: "Many Methodists would disapprove of a minister sitting in a tavern being accepted by the patrons as one of themselves. They would feel that there was something wrong in a minister being there at all. Yet I cannot help but feel that this is where we would find our Master, the carpenter's son, if he were here in the flesh to-day." Our simplest actions belie our faith. And the language we use in church distorts it out of recognition. Much of our religious and most of our theological language is an affront to men. This is not because it is unintelligible but because it is clearly seen to be a smoke screen to hide the love and joy and command of Jesus.

Our church buildings, especially those for weekday use, are commonly thought of as having no connection with the weekday affairs of the people of the neighborhood. They are generally regarded, both by those inside the church and those without, as being for the exclusive use of the members of the church. Would it not be a good thing to break down this exclusiveness in the use of buildings: for church meetings to be held in "secular" buildings — in the village or town hall — in schools — and not because the church hall is not big enough, but of intention, to demonstrate that the church belongs to the neighborhood; and for the church halls to be made available regularly for secular organizations? Is it good that the church hall and the community center should be thought of as intended for different kinds of activities, though carried out by the same people? If there were less distinction between the things that could and the things that could not be done in a church hall and a real interchange of place of meeting, there would be more of a sense that people matter more than activities and that all the people of the neighborhood belong to the church, at least in the eyes of the church and in its care.

The local church is called on to express its love to its immediate neighbors, without discrimination. It has also a duty to demonstrate to its immediate neighbors that all men are their neighbors. It has to witness to a love limitless in width and depth. The church expresses this in all its acts of worship, and must express this also in its corporate acts of service. In many cases the local church can do this in token ways — in raising money for interchurch aid, in taking part in propaganda for the removal of racial injustices, in entertaining strangers. But what it declares in its worship it must somehow demonstrate to its immediate neighbors.

It is only as all this is evident in the content of its worship and in the intention of its corporate activities that the activities of its individual members can have meaning and find support. The witness of the church is not made within the church but in the ordinary lay world around. It is made effective by the actions of its members in that lay, secular world which is their own.

In this context of the life of the local church to which they belong we can go on to think of the particular tasks that await the layman in his inescapable day-to-day contact with his neighbors. He can never escape from this, for from the nature of his life and work he can never escape contact with other men. But, apart from this casual contact with neighbors in which interest and courtesy are the common currency of Christian love, there are three aspects of the life of his community in which the layman has to act deliberately. These three necessary lines of activity in social life are: (1) personal participation in political life, without which a democracy cannot survive; (2) a sharing in the common corporate social activities of his neighborhood, which provide the soil in which alone political democracy can grow; and (3) personal concern in all those forms of expression — of the arts, entertainment, and propaganda — through which human values are handed on and developed and that joy expressed without which life loses any touch of glory and becomes boring. Along these three lines of social activity in his neighborhood the layman has to make his conscious and deliberate contribution. It is obvious that no one person can make an equal contribution along all three lines. It may well be that a man or woman is so involved in one that he has no time for the others. But the combined contribution of the laity in the area must effectively operate in all three.

Nothing has been more indicative of the tragic decline of the lay life of the church in Britain than the way in which church people have dropped out of political life in the last fifty years. We have already mentioned this in Chapters 3 and 5, and seen something of its cause in the adoption of the minister-figure as the model Christian. Fifty years ago the leaders of local political life were also prominent in the service of their local church. For example, fifty years ago the elders of a Scottish church took a leading part in local and party politics. Today the same church, in all probability, a much larger kirk session will be found. Almost certainly there will have been extensive additions to the old hall, because the organizations will have increased in number and size. In every way the church will be more efficiently organized and more of its members will be spending more of their time on church premises. But it will be rare to find that one of the elders or officers is a member of the town council or on the committee of a political party. This is true in the west end and in the east end of our cities and is as true of England as of Scotland. It is not so true of the smaller towns and the rural areas, where the older life of a rural neighborhood still survives.

We can find particular reasons for this revolutionary change, in addition to the example of the minister. The church was slow to realize what was happening in the world and to adjust its thinking to new parties and policies. This was due largely to the failure of the church to think in economic terms and therefore to face the coming issues of the time. There were perhaps more respectable, theological reasons — in a new emphasis on the mission of the church rather than on the personal obedience of Christians, in the popularity of a church-centered theology, in a greater concern for the efficiency of the organization and administration of the church, and, perhaps, even in a new glimpse of the need for training church members.

But, however respectable the reasons, the result has been the withdrawal of the laity from active and responsible participation in political life. This, of course, is not to say that there are not innumerable church members in political life. It is to say that the present lay leaders of the local church are not engaged in politics, as were their fathers and grandfathers, and that the church members who are so engaged are looked at askance by the church for not giving their time to the affairs of the church.

The members of the church would find justification for this attitude by saying: "There is so much to do in the church"; or "Church work must come first," or "If you go into politics, you must take sides and a Christian must be impartial and not take sides," or "You'll split the church. We must have nothing controversial in the church," or "How are we to decide what side is right? We don't know the facts"; "Politics is a dirty game; Christians must keep their hands clean."

These are arguments that might have a certain cogency in the mouth of a minister, but they are odd comments to come from a layman. A clergyman can claim that he is paid to do the church's work and that the work for which he is paid must come first. He may feel that he must not let any of his other interests prejudice his work. He may feel that he should not participate in party politics. He will indeed, if he is a minister of the Church of England or of the Church of Scotland, be disqualified from full participation by the law of the country. He may claim, and with some excuse, that he has not that knowledge of secular life which would enable him to make decisions on certain subjects. He may and often does take shelter behind these reasons and excuses.

But the layman denies his laity if he uses such arguments.

For none of these applies to *him* in his own job and in his ordinary contacts with men.

In his daily life, whatever his occupation, he has always to be committed daily to make decisions and to take sides. Whether he be manager or worker, he is bound to be in a particular situation with specialized, one-sided knowledge. He has got to think out his duty in terms of his work and its demands and in the light of the opposing demands and claims of others. He is never in a position where he is quite unbiased and can see all sides equally fairly and with no selfish interest of his own.

He has daily to make decisions on the facts as he sees them. Indeed, the value of his opinion and the truth of his decisions depend on his one-sided knowledge of one particular thing — his job.

And are the jobs in which men work for their daily bread so much cleaner than the work of politics? Are men not in their jobs partly, but always, for what they get out of them? Could many work if they got no pay? What does it mean to say that politics is a dirty game? That you have to compromise to get things done? That men are ambitious and want to make a name for themselves and therefore to push ahead of others? Is this true only of politics? Is there any business or profession, including the full-time service of the church, to which it does not apply? Why is politics alone a dirty game, unless we are looking for an excuse to keep out and want the political setup to remain as it is — at least for our day?

The peculiar contribution that the layman can make to the political life of his country is that his experience of ordinary secular life is combined with a serious view of the material world as the creation of God and the conviction that in Jesus Christ — in his life, death, and resurrection — is given the way of the world's working and the hope of its glory and that, therefore, he brings to political life both experience and love. It is this combination which makes him a layman. And if these two things are not combined, he can be a menace: either a starry-eyed idealist or a sanctimonious self-seeker.

In actual fact the layman today is probably as much deterred from active participation in local political life by the arduous nature of the work involved and the poorness of the reward, as by the more ecclesiastic reasons mentioned above. Political life at all levels and not least at its lowest level is a matter of patient dealing with other people's problems, of mastering dull facts and enduring the endless tedium of committees. This is particularly true of local political life, which for most people is the beginning of political activity. This is the hidden, unrewarded, altruistic work on which a democracy depends. The health of a democracy depends on the willingness of a great number of its citizens to serve on voluntary and statutory bodies, on their willingness to learn and to teach; and on the devotion and integrity of its officials. This is the world in which the layman is peculiarly called to serve, for this is his world and he brings to it the gifts required: patience, perseverance, attention to the needs of others, and a willingness to deal with individual cases.

Involvement in the political life of the neighborhood is taken first, as it is the basis of the political life of the nation. Concern with the political problems of a neighborhood — industry, housing, education, and the rest — leads inevitably into wider issues, national and international. The wider aspects of the layman's political responsibility have been dealt with in the previous chapter. It is important here to remember that this begins in a man's neighborhood. It is important also to beware of the cynicism so often expressed by church people about local and national government. Anger, opposition, revolt, are political emotions hallowed by the Bible. The cynicism that is content to criticize and to do nothing is deadly — for the church.

The vitality of a community's life depends also upon the kind of corporate life that people are enjoying in the informal contacts and activities of the neighborhood. How does a community weave that network of relationships and social skills and amusements without which there can be no kind of social life and so no training for political life? There are firstly the natural relationships of kin and the imposed relationships of work. Without these there would be no social structure at all. Without the demands of hunger and developing needs demanding satisfaction, there would be no possibility of corporate life. But the attempt to find meaning in this social life depends upon the activities in which people engage from pleasure and choice. These develop from the things people do from necessity. The hunt, undertaken to find food, takes on the nature of sport. The production of necessities develops into creation of art. This form of social life, expressed in games, entertainment, and all the multitude of interests that bring men together, is an essential part of the life of men. It is for work that man is created in the image of God; and he is placed in the garden "to till it and keep it," as Genesis puts it. And a man's work is what makes his life. But it is in the activities of their leisure that men find how to express the meaning of their life. In an age when the process of work has become more impersonal, the activities of leisure attain a new significance. Leisure provides opportunity for self-chosen activities and is therefore of immense importance in a society where a man's work is increasingly planned and ordered. But these leisure-time activities are of importance not only for the health of the individual; they are also the means by which he is brought into free association and cooperation with his neighbors. The football field, the bowling alley, the dramatic society, and the restaurant are of great value to the community as places where people meet and do things together. So are shops and parks and buses. So too are the places where people meet together as spectators — movie theaters, concerts, and games. These informal meeting places are the nurseries of political life, capable of all kinds of influence, for good and evil.

The church has in the last centuries been detached from this side of the life of a neighborhood. The so-called Puritan tradition has made it suspicious of games and entertainment. Now that that influence has disappeared from the lives of the members of the church, the church has tended to regard games and amusements as individual activities in which its members find relaxation; and to tolerate them unless they bring people together in rivalry to church services or activities. The church has failed to see these social activities as worthwhile and of value in their own right.

Today when the old, close neighborhood has gone and social activities can no longer be thought of in terms of the village green, we should be concerned with new ways in which corporate activities, both sporting and artistic, can be developed. In the days when the wealthy individual was the patron of the arts it was natural that the interest of the arts should be largely individualistic. Today when the patrons are increasingly public bodies, it is to be hoped that artistic concern should be more social. And in this the church must have a part both as a public patron and through its members as they participate in all the corporate activities of their community.

All this is vital for the recovery of meaning in urban life. The church, having never deliberately taken industry into its thinking, has never accepted the modern industrial life as the world in which it lives out the gospel. It sees the rural parish as the place where it belongs and where it is at home. It does, indeed, see the place of the cathedral city or the university town or the old market town, for in them the old pattern of life has not been too visibly disturbed. The parish system of the national churches of Britain, which has ensured that the church cannot abandon the centers of the cities and industrial towns, disguises rather than prevents the failure of the church. The American "downtown" areas reveal the true abandonment of the city by the churches. There it has been indeed exaggerated by the removal of the well-to-do into the wide expanses of their suburbs and by the occupation of the abandoned centers by immigrants and the underprivileged. But the problem is essentially the same in Britain. The neighborhood people want is the immediate, if not too close, company of those of similar income, background, and interests. They want the suburb not only because it gives something of the health and peace of the old half-remembered village life but also because it is a means of escaping from the city, from the place of work and of conflicting contracts, and from that wider and more demanding neighborhood that is man's world today. The church, with its inheritance of the parish system and its dream of a small, closely knit congregation, has helped this. To the church the center of the city has not been the place where its life and witness have been most evident. Instead it has been "the city of dreadful night," from which it had to rescue men.

To seek to reconstruct villages in the cities of today is just as hopeless a task for the church as it is for social planners. The task of the church is to begin to consider what the life of a city should be. It cannot do this unless it begins to understand the modern structure of our society and its organization industrially and governmentally in large units. In the last century the church failed to meet the needs of the new industrial society by failing to give any help to those engaged in industry. In the same way the church failed to meet adequately the problems and the opportunities of life in the new industrial towns by thinking only in terms of parishes which had become meaningless boundaries on a map. We reap the harvest now in town areas that have little in community life except in the supporting of their local football teams, and in a church that exists precariously on the fringe of local life. The church must realize that the city is the form of man's social life. But it will not be able to do this unless its members begin to feel their identification as Christians with the life of their fellow citizens and to find not only their duty but their pleasure in doing things with them and so quite deliberately try to find the way to a fuller, more purposeful life for a city.

We have stressed the importance of the neglected city neighborhood for two reasons. One is that the city or town is the place of life and work for most laymen and will become increasingly so. The other reason is that it is here that the layman is called to a task that is new in its circumstances and demands. The layman will have to begin to think in quite a new way and with a fresh sense of responsibility about the kind of life he wants to live with all his neighbors in his town or city. He will have to begin to think of the life of his city or town as a whole. He will have to take a much more active part in the secular affairs of his city, both in civic duties and in corporate entertainments. He will need to go on to consider the problems that affect the life of the city not from the point of view of how proposed solutions will affect the church but of how they will promote or hinder the development of a sense of corporate life in the city, especially in its center. These questions include the provision of recreational and cultural centers, Sunday observance, licensing regulations. We are inclined to regard these as urgent questions only insofar as they effect what we call the "problems of youth." But the problem of youth is basically that there is in our cities and towns no adequate adult social life into which they can enter.

There is the urgent problem that the church faces in the centers of our cities among those still living there in decayed and depressing slum conditions and among those who gravitate to the center because there alone the streets give hint of some life — the transient, the hopeless, and the depraved. The church in various ways does try to tackle this problem (which is essentially the old parish problem writ large and without the resources of a large congregation). The problem we are considering here is wider, not so obviously urgent in terms of blighted lives and the health of children, but ultimately perhaps more urgent if our cities are not to become well-planned and well-built dormitories of men and women who don't know why they are there and hopelessly plan to retire to a countryside where they are even more bored.

There are profound theological implications in the growth of cities. As Michael Jackson, the leader of the Sheffield Industrial Mission, has said: "The Bible starts in a garden and ends in a city; the city is the place for the working out of God's purpose for the defeat of idolatry and social injustice. . . . The theological question is: What is God saying to the Churches through their defeat in urban society and through the new urban culture? The Church is confronted with a new secular urban civilization in order that Christians may find again their lay obedience in the world."

So the church has to think out its mission in the new urban society which is already ours and which will inevitably develop, if it has the time to develop, into a more highly industrialized, more unified society with more education and more leisure available for its members. It must do so not merely in the old terms of the parish, though there are still the claims of the physical neighborhood, but in terms of the city as a whole. In this task the layman has his part to play. Indeed it could more truly be said that this is his task in which he has to give the lead, for it is a new area for the church's concern. In this the laity have a unique contribution to make to society and to the church.

This leads naturally to the third aspect of the layman's task in his neighborhood. Political responsibility and social involvement come first. There is a third which may seem less urgent and which indeed can be dealt with only briefly here. This third aspect is the part played in our society by the spoken and the acted word, by music and art, now offered to all through radio and television; and the part that Christians should play in this world where art and propaganda intertwine. This business of communication has a vital and radically new place in the life of a community. It is new in that for the first time there is a practical means of speaking to all who are not deaf, whether they can read or not. It is new, too, in that elementary education has seen to it that very few cannot read. It is new, too, in that the old cultural divisions between classes, typified by the old distinction of theater and music hall, have been broken down. There is the possibility of popular culture. Plenty of problems remain. The principal one is of control. In the past, individuals controlled art and communication — the king, the nobles, the church. They controlled it by their greater learning, by their wealth, and by their power. The problem remains for us in a different form. Who will control our news and art? Who will use them for their own ends? How can a responsible community take charge?

The church is very much involved in all this. In the past it had great power to develop or control art and always it has used the art of words. To the outside world it is the oldest and largest agent of propaganda in the world. The church would not see itself in this way as involved in the business of advertisement and propaganda. It has tended to regard art and propaganda as harmful, not because of this rivalry for the souls of men but because they did not represent the truth. The church today has to rethink its attitude toward art and communication. It has to become interested in the whole business of corporate art and of common means of communication. It has to do so if it is to be heard by men.

But its need goes farther than this. Art has always been

the second interpreter of the gospel. The life lived by Christians is the first. The interpretation of this life, insofar as it reached interested outsiders, is not through theology which is at first intelligible only to those inside, but through art, through the drawing, the cartoon, the diagram, the dance, the action. Even in places where the gospel is still something that seems familiar, it is not the words of the preacher or the writings of the theologian, or even the life of the member of the church, that makes the first impression on the outsider. It is the church building — or, if he enters the church, it is the furniture and the windows. It is the work of architect and builder, of carpenter and artist. This is what the casual outsider sees; and the pictures in books and in shopwindows — all the varied and sometimes distorted vision of Christmas cards, texts, and notice boards. In this quite material way the church's first contact with most people outside is always through the arts.

In all these spheres of primary contact with people the layman must be the agent. The jobs of architect, builder, carpenter, and artist are lay jobs and they are professional jobs. Does the church see the architects and craftsmen it uses as the pioneers of its mission? Does it see actors and painters as laymen committed to the expression of their faith in their own way? Does it see them as in the church at all?

This may be the test of the church's acceptance of the laity. For these — the artists — are the quintessence of laity. Their faith is expressed in their work. They are generally so truly single-minded in their devotion to their art that they cannot be what the church so often wants them to be — laymen in their leisure time. They have a vital role to play in the creation of a new community life in our cities. Their work demands the cooperation of others. It is for these reasons that this matter of art and communication is the third and vital aspect of the task of the layman in his neighborhood.

7. *The Layman and the Local Church*

In previous chapters we have considered the tasks of the layman in his daily work, in his neighborhood, and in his political responsibilities, national and international. In this chapter we think of his place in the local church; of his work there.

It may seem strange that we should take this after the others. Should this chapter not have come first? When we think of a layman are we not thinking of someone who is primarily a member of the church? Is it not in the local church that he essentially belongs? Is it not here that he has to learn to do his work before he can go out into the world outside the church to do Christian work there?

Why, indeed, do we take it last? Precisely because we generally would put it first. We often seem to think that it is in the local church that the church member primarily belongs. We see him as beginning his Christian life in the local church. We see the local church as the sufficient area for his obedience. Too often his Christian activity is seen as bounded by the walls of the local church building and his Christian life as confined within a congregation. And this is not true in history or in theology.

The life of a Christian does indeed begin with his baptism into the church. But the church into which he is baptized is not the building, nor is it the congregation that worships in the building. There is nothing in the New Testament to suggest that such an idea was ever in the minds of the apostles or of the early church. The convert was baptized into Christ — into his body: the one church throughout the world, the one holy catholic and apostolic church. And by the miracle of God's providence this truth has been preserved by all the broken fragments of the church. However divided they may be in their practice and interpretation of Holy Communion, the historic churches are united in confessing that there is only one baptism and that baptism is the one means of admission into the church.

The one church into which a child or an adult is baptized is not contained in buildings, however essential they may be, nor is it confined to the congregation that uses the buildings, even though that congregation is the only visible manifestation of the church in his locality, and its fellowship the necessary framework for his growth. The church into which he is baptized is much larger than this. It cannot be contained in buildings or confined to institutions. It is something both simpler and more mysterious, more indefinite and yet more comprehensible to men; it is the body of Christ, the whole body of his people. It is God who builds the church, and its stones are men and women. The action of God in creating the church is as mysterious and as basic to the faith and as much an article of faith as his action in the creation of the world and in the coming of Jesus Christ. And the nature and purpose of the church cannot be different from God's purpose in the creation and incarnation. Just as the Bible declares that this mess of a world, with all the cruelty and injustice that the Old Testament knew so well, is created by God and sings his praise; just as he comes to us in one who was born of a woman, was tempted in all points like as we are, and died as a criminal on a cross and is yet the King of Glory, risen and ascended: so the church is made up of ordinary men and women, yet is, by God's action, his Son's body on earth, living his life, doing his will, knowing his glory. And, as his body, it is here in the world to be the instrument of God's purpose for the world.

It is into this church that a man is brought by baptism: into this society of men and women which is Christ's body on earth. It is because it is into this church that he is brought and because this church is set in the world to be the bearer of God's love to the world that we have discussed first a Christian's duty in the world—in his work, his neighborhood, his world—before we go on to discuss his work in the local manifestation of the church which is the place of his training and his home. His primary task as a Christian is in the world insofar as he is part of the church called to preach the kingdom and heal the sick. And these are actions that have meaning in the world and not in the church.

Enough has surely been said, and by enough people, to make it unnecessary to repeat that the church is not a building. Even though our common usage still equates the building with the church, we all agree that the church is the people. But have we knocked down the bogey of the church as the building, only to put the congregation in its place? We think of the church as being the people who worship in the church building, whose duty it is to use it and whose responsibility it is to maintain it, who talk about the building as "our church," who are in truth the tenants of the building. Is this way of thinking any better than thinking of the building as the church? When we talk about the church as the people of God we mean something larger than this.

Buildings are necessary and some organization of God's people is essential if the church is to do its work in the world. But these are secondary and ancillary: as tools and a house are necessary for life but are not life itself. It is the life of Christ in the church that makes the church. Jesus never built a building nor organized an institution. What he did was to call men to live his life. Of the eternal truth of this life the Sacraments are the sign and seal. Its life is a life of obedience, but unless it knows the source of love and joy and peace it can never truly obey or make its witness attractive and challenging to men. It knows that all it does is for the glory of God and to his praise. In this it echoes the praise and joy that Jesus always expressed. In this it enters into the praise that all creation offers to God, and expresses that praise on the behalf of all men and all things. And in its praise it offers praise on its own behalf — praise to God for Jesus himself and for all his benefits. This is the only thing that the church can do in its own right and in its own name. The glory of the church is that it knows why it offers its praise — in its life, its service, and its worship, and where two or three meet in the name of Jesus, there is the church.

This is why worship is the peculiar duty of the church, and why men have said that the whole duty of the church is to offer worship to God. This is true, if we remember that *this worship is expressed in all we do and not only in our special acts of worship*. For the church is not the only place where men can worship God. They can worship him in the work of their hands, in their solitary prayers, and in their corporate activities.

And the place of worship is not the place of witness or of work. It is not the primary place for the preaching of the gospel or for the healing of the sick. Paul knew that the place for the preaching of the gospel was the marketplace and even the prison. The work of preaching and of healing had to go on outside, wherever men were. The work of preaching could go on effectively only where men could ask questions and discuss. We have today come to the strange position that the normal preaching of the Word is seen as the special performance of professionally trained men in a building where questions and discussion are forbidden. This is to confuse the work and the worship of the church; to identify the teaching of those inside with the proclamation of the Word to the world.

The church nevertheless has to find some way of organizing its life. The forms it has found have changed through the centuries according to the structure of society and the peculiar tasks of the church at any time: the household of the first three Christian centuries, the convent of the Middle Ages, the family of the Reformation and Counter-Reformation — these have been some of the very different forms in which the church has organized its life. The congregation is the pattern we accept today, but there is nothing permanent in any of these forms. Indeed the form must always be changing if the church is to live. Of course some form of corporate Christian living is necessary if the church is to nourish, train, and uphold its members for and in that work which is the full life and witness of the church. It is for this that all the ministries, offices, and organizations of the church exist, as Paul so clearly states in his letter to the Ephesians: "And these were his gifts: some to be apostles, some prophets, some evangelists, some pastors and teachers, to equip God's people for work in his service, to the building up of the body of Christ" (Eph. 4:11–12, NEB.)

In the local church — in its life and worship — what is the layman's place and function? Though the local church is not the limit of his activities and loyalties, it has its necessary place in his life and he has his peculiar function in it.

He has his part to play in its worship; and this part is not a merely passive one. It is not sufficient to say that he should attend public worship every Sunday and partake of Holy Communion so many times a year. Undoubtedly there is some value in attendance and something sometimes to be gained from being attentive. But too often the layman feels that all that is demanded of him in worship is that he attend and be attentive. And this can be the end of worship for him. But worship can be a means of grace only as a man feels that worship is something that he, with others, does, and not something he watches and listens to the parson doing. One of the healthiest signs of liturgical revival in the church is the way in which the people are being helped to find their part in the worship of the church: not by doing things that the minister used to do, though there are many actions in worship that should be given back to the laity, but in appreciating and being trained in the parts of the service that have always been theirs.

But the intelligent participation of the laity in the worship of the local church depends on more than this. Inevitably worship must always depend to a very great extent on the man to whom is committed the function of leading the worship of the people. But his task in leading worship corresponds more to that of the conductor of an orchestra than to that of a soloist. Even if his is the only voice to be heard, he is still leading the united worship of many—or preventing it. And often he is preventing it. It is naturally very difficult for the clergyman to appreciate the frustration of many laymen and therefore to understand why so many laymen who claim to be keen churchmen are yet often not to be found at public worship, and why many more have entirely lapsed from any even irregular attendance.

There are two main reasons for this frustration. The first is that the layman wants to feel that he is doing something positive with his experience, while often all that is asked of him in worship is that he be attentive. A parson finds this difficult to appreciate—at least until he takes up some extraparochial work and joins the laity in worship. Then he can appreciate as never before the real frustration of many laity in worship—and the fact that often their only means of expressing their frustrations is to stay away!

The other cause is the language of the clergy. When Paul used words like "redemption" or "bought with a price" he was using the secular, or rather the pagan, language of the men of his time. He explained the faith in terms of freedom because slavery was the common economic and social problem of his time. We have made the language of theology and of our worship the academic language of the library and study, which men have to be trained to understand and are not often trained to interpret. How would Paul interpret the faith if he were living today? Certainly not in terms of slavery and redemption or of a pagan psychology, but in terms in which men talk today — of atoms and energy, or war and peace. The language of our theology and worship makes the layman inattentive and, in the end, absent. Dr. Roy Pearson, Dean of Andover Newton Theological School, quotes a French minister who felt that nowadays: "He no longer faces a congregation of the saved wanting to be sent, but an audience of the lost whose hope of being found grows fainter." Or consider this quotation from the *British Weekly* in a comment on the unintelligibility of what has been called "ecumenical English": "People with a passion for the right use of words could help the churches. A few philosophers and journalists could clean up language which, in its own way, is just as dirty as any blasphemies or oaths which the coarse layman may utter."

The layman is not content now merely to attend the worship of his local church. He knows that if the worship is to be worship for him he must participate. And participation means contribution. The minister holds the key to this, because his is the responsibility for the conduct of worship, and therefore the responsibility of finding the means for greater and more effective lay participation in worship. This is indeed what it means to say that he "leads" the worship of the church.

The position is altered when we consider the place of the layman in the organizational life of the local church. In this *he* holds the key. The purpose of the organizations of the church is to nourish and train the members of the church for their work in the world and to uphold them in it. Here the relationship of clergy and laity are the opposite of their relationship in worship. In worship the minister is the trained man and the man in authority. The laity have their share and creative responsibility in worship but depend basically on the peculiar authority of the clergy. In the sphere of local action, the layman is the one with the wider experience and the greater authority, though the minister also shares in this sphere of public and social responsibility. He is a citizen as much as any layman is, and has his lay responsibilities. His greater opportunities for study should lead him to a deeper understanding of some issues. But from the wider responsibilities and tensions of secular life he is excluded. He is excluded from the life of production and distribution, from the discipline of the legal and medical professions: indeed from the ordinary secular working world which is the life of the laity. If to certain matters he brings the virtue of detachment, for most others he lacks the relevance of experience. We should perhaps remember that in this the celibate clergy are sometimes in a better position than the married clergy. Where the clergy are celibate they are of necessity all the sons of laymen. Where the clergy marry, we run the risk of clerical families who know little of secular life.

It will, of course, be argued that the life of any particular layman may be very much more restricted than the minister's. Each layman's experience is limited to his particular job and interests. His range may indeed be very narrow. But, narrow as it is, it belongs to a world into which the minister cannot enter and where he can give no lead. In the sphere of action the laity cannot look to the clergy for leadership as they can in the sphere of worship — that is, if the action is to be in the world and not just in the church building.

This is where the laity have to find for themselves a new sense of responsibility. Here they are in real difficulty. They are always waiting for a lead from the clergy. But such help as has been given in their devotional life, both Catholic and Protestant, has tended to exalt clerical above lay life. Its language and its example have been in terms of clerical virtue and clerical action. The effect of all this has been to

make the layman feel that he is indeed a second-class Christian — a listener and an imitator, not an initiator or a doer.
Somehow, this order has to be reversed.

Indeed, the first duty of the layman in his local church is to be a nuisance. This is not easy for him, for all the teaching that he has received in the church from his childhood is that he should be modest, self-effacing, accommodating, and obedient — in fact, everything but a nuisance. He has got to be a nuisance in asking questions: "Why do we do this or that in church?" "What does the minister mean when he says such and such?" He should be a nuisance in demanding and suggesting action on all kinds of lines, in church and outside. He has got to be a persistent nuisance, for everything will be done to silence him or disregard him.

When we say that the layman should be a nuisance in his local church, we do not mean that he should be so simply in order to criticize and find fault. The awkwardness of his questions and demands must arise from his conviction that as a member of the church he is called to the exercise of an active virtue, from a dissatisfaction with what the church seems to be asking of him, and also from a perception that there are certain directions along which he ought to be traveling but isn't.

The first idea that has to be challenged is the commonly accepted view of the relation of the congregation to the parish. In the Church of England and the Church of Scotland there is a lot of glib talk about being the parish church and of the unbreakable tie that binds the church to the parish and of the church's responsibility for the life of all in the parish. It is not this idea which we challenge. It expresses a truth and it has prevented in Britain the almost total abandonment of the inner city by the churches, which is so distressing a feature of America, where the churches have felt that their tie was not to the locality but to the congregation — and so when the people moved to the suburbs the churches moved with them. What is to be criticized in Britain is the superficiality of this parish conception as it survives. Responsibility seems to have shrunk to an obligation to perform certain functions for those in the parish — baptisms, marriages, funerals. So often the name "parish church" disguises a congregational life as self-centered as can be found in any gathered congregation. This narrow conception of the relationship of the congregation to the locality in which it is set has to be challenged. The congregation has to find a new expression of its identity with, and responsibility for, the secular life around it. This can only be achieved if it is primarily in terms of the laity.

A second challenge follows from this and has been referred to already in Chapter 3: the generally accepted idea that the life and activities of a congregation revolve round the minister and that it is he who determines what the members do and think has to be overturned. The clergy may well protest that they have no desire that this should be so, but the idea is so generally accepted and is so convenient for all parties that it will need something in the nature of a revolt to overturn it. This revolt can be carried out only by the laity.

The third idea that has to be dissolved is linked with the previous one. This is the commonly accepted idea that nothing should be done in a congregation unless it is an activity open to all. The argument is that there should not be in the congregation any cliques or groups with special interests that exclude others, or if you must have them, they should be only for leisure-time activities such as softball and remain, in any case, of questionable value. Any group that was concerned with more fundamental interests would be suspect as leading to division among the members. And so long as everything in the congregation is seen as dependent on the minister, it will be to his convenience, and certainly to his comfort, to discourage anything that divides the congregation. But if there is to be a full expression of the total interests and concerns of the laity, there must be a departure from this idea that there is one kind of life common to all lay men and women.

There is no one layman's job to balance the parson's job. Behind the hesitation to accept differentiation in the concerns and activities of the members of a church is the desire to find this one elusive layman's job. This is but another example of the domination of the idea of the minister over the idea of the laity. The parson's job, for all the differences of office to which he may be called, is one job, for which all go through the same kind of training. The common nature of this job transcends denominational differences and makes it easier for them to talk to one another than to other men. This is far from being so with the layman. There is no occupation common to laymen. There is no language common to laymen unless by "lay" we mean simply "nonclerical." In most churches the number of occupations represented will be surprisingly high. The members differ in jobs, in training, in specialist experience and knowledge in a way unknown among the clergy.

The nearest approach to one lay job is to be found among the women of the church, who are indeed more than half of the laity. The largest group among them have one job in common — that of caring for their homes. This is the one job that the church has recognized fully as the job of the laity. This is why it is this group of women — married women or single women spending their time in the running of their homes — who at the moment very largely make up the active laity of the church. Their job has been recognized. The reason why women in professional and commercial life are not so obvious in church and why so few men are in church at all is that their jobs have not been recognized.

The idea that there is the one layman's job and therefore no need for any differentiation between members in the life and work of the church has to be abandoned if the church is to express its faith in action in the life of its members in the world. There can be serious concern with the diverse gifts and experiences of men and women in the church only if opportunity is found for the existence of particular local or specialized groups in a congregation. If this differentiation is not made and the church continues to find some one common job for the layman parallel to the minister's, this will be expressed, and cannot but be expressed, in terms of the layman's service in the church buildings, and will be inevitably interpreted in terms of assisting the full-time minister. There is a place, and an important place, for the laity in the business of the local church. But if our concern about the ministry of the laity is confined to this, the church will be worse off than when men asked no questions about their tasks as church people. For if this is seen as the one ministry of the laity, there will be fewer and fewer laity in the church; for there is only a limited number of service jobs waiting to be done in any congregation, and those who are unused or unusable will feel that there is nothing for them to do, that they are unwanted, and they will fall away.

There is, however, one bit of work inside the congregation which is different in kind from the maintenance of the fabric and institution of the church, and which in a peculiar way depends on the laity — or, at least, on some of them. This is the work of training the next generation — the work of education in the church.

We have seen how the Sunday school of the last century was the pioneer of the new pattern of life in the church: how it led to the building of halls and to the development of activities for its older members who were suffering equally from the collapse of the old rural family pattern of life. In those days the church did what it could through Sunday schools for those who had no chance of education. Today its task is very different. The church has to offer education to children and young people for whom the opportunity of education is universal and compulsory and who at the same time are open to the influence of other teaching than the church's in a way unknown before. The task of the education of the children of the church is therefore a much more difficult one than it was in the past. It demands trained people. These trained people are obviously lay people. This is a specialist lay job in the church, demanding much more consideration than is often given to it.

This is essential. But the biggest contribution to the Christian training of children and young people is not made by these specialists but by the congregation as a whole.

The purpose of all our schemes for the education of the young of the church is their incorporation into the life of the church. The single greatest cause of the church's failure in the training of its young — and the reason why so many who have been at Sunday school and in the youth organizations are rarely seen afterward in church — is that there is *no full, demanding, and attractive life into which to be incorporated.* The formal and informal education that children receive in church is basically an interpretation of the life of the church. If this life which is shown to them has obviously little to do with the life they see their parents and the other members of the church live, they are not likely to regard this church life as important. They know that it is irrelevant even when they receive instruction as children. They assert their liberty to have done with irrelevant things when they gain power to choose for themselves.

If children can see — and this is manifestly true in many cases — that what they are learning in church does explain how their parents and the other people they know in church live, and the choices and decisions they make, then this teaching becomes relevant and indeed exciting. They are learning the values and codes of behavior of the society to which they know they belong and into which they want fully to enter, when they grow up. They must know the life of the church as purposeful and attractive, and must indeed know this life as their own before they can be confirmed into it.

But this depends on this life being indeed the life that the adults of the church are obviously living or trying to live. This is why the most important contribution to the Christian education of the young is made by the congregation as a whole. It is here that the church seems to be failing. Children and young people are not often aware of the reality of Christian living in the church. They do not see it, even if it is there. Indeed, rather are they aware that the choices and decisions of their parents and of the adults of the church are made on other grounds than those of Christian love and service. It is the contradiction between what they are taught in church and school, and adult life as they see it, that makes the gap between youth and the church. The development of a full, adult, responsible, and corporate life in the church is essential for the education of the young, and this is the primary contribution to the training of the young which the laity must make.

At present, the life of the congregation, with of course some exceptions, is neither full nor adult, neither responsible nor corporate. Its present organization prevents it from being any of these.

Let us take them in turn.

The present life of the church is not a full life. The members of the church as they participate in the life of the church do not do so fully as persons. It may be that as they join in the worship of the church they, by the grace of God, join fully as persons: that as they confess their sins and ask for forgiveness, as they ask for light and strength and make their intercessions, they bring, insofar as they are able all the failures and anxieties, all their concerns and commitments of their fuller and private lives. There is no doubt that this is so. Otherwise few would worship. But insofar as the church accepts them into its life and activities it, as it were, expects them to leave part of their lives outside. And the part that is left outside is the part that is the most worrying — their life of business and politics. In the life of the church they participate not as full people but as those who perform certain functions. It is by their usefulness to the church that they are valued. They are officers, or teachers in the Sunday school, or members of the choir, or, at the very bottom, attenders or poor attenders. This way of speech indicates how narrow is the common conception of the life of the church. It is generally confined to the activities needed to maintain the organization. It is not a life embracing all that rich and variegated and confusing life which is the life lived by the members of the church — and therefore hardly touching the life of those outside. It is only as men and women — and children — are regarded fully as persons and all their concerns brought into the life of the church that the life of the church can be said to be full.

Another way of saying it is to say that the life of the church is not adult, for what is excluded are the concerns of adult life. We have seen how the congregational pattern of life in the church began with the care of children and went on to provide leisure-time activities for adults deprived of family life. Its program is still apt to be confined to religious education and leisure activities. There has been, since the Second World War, a considerable widening of the range of topics that can be discussed in church organizations. But the conviction that controversial topics should not be discussed is still strong, and even stronger is the idea that the two topics that have no place in the life of the church are work and politics. But these, together with sex, are the main concerns of adult life. The church is certainly aware of sex, and in the main still deals with it by a conventional silence. Its treatment of work and politics has been that of unawareness. Men and women are, however, concerned in their daily lives mainly with questions arising out of their jobs and with questions of their relationship with their neighbors, near and far. The exclusion of industry and politics from the daily life of the church is the main reason why men and women engaged in these spheres are the groups most conspicuous for their absence from church today.

So the life of the congregation is not a responsible life. It is not training and exercising its members in Christian responsibility. Responsibility resides in making decisions and taking action. This is something that a congregation is not accustomed to do except in some carefully regulated ecclesiastical affairs. Its duty is to attend, to listen, to be instructed. Today the church begins to see that this is not enough. Opportunities are sought for the members of the congregation to ask questions, to study, to discuss. Such opportunities are limited and apt to be poorly supported. This is because they are purposeless. They are not expected to result in decision and action. Discussion must cover all points of view. It must be impartial. But decision is never impartial and action is only possible along one line at a time. Discussion can range from China to Peru and maintain the high-minded impartiality of the irresponsible. Responsibility involves the necessity of choosing one line of action, of committing oneself to it, of taking one's stand alongside other people. The life of the congregation does not train people to do this. Indeed, it prevents people from doing this by suggesting that to have a Christian standpoint is enough and that the political duty of a Christian is confined to criticizing other people and, above all, questioning their motives.

It is, of course, not the place of the church to make decisions on matters on which its members are not informed, nor to take action on all issues. It is its duty to see that its members are being trained and accustomed to making their own Christian decisions and taking their own actions in their own public and private lives. This it is not doing. By its present pattern of life it makes its members avoid decisions and fear action. Men and women can only learn how to make decisions and take action if they are making real decisions and taking real action in the affairs of their church and its local responsibilities. But such decisions and action should be those which affect their own daily lives. The most important decisions of our lives concern how we spend our time and how we spend our money; for no action can be taken that does not affect our time or our money. It is in these questions that the members of a congregation have to learn corporate and individual responsibility.

And because the life of a congregation is neither fully personal, nor adult, nor responsible it cannot be said to be truly corporate. At its best it is merely sociable. It allows some of its members the opportunity of doing some things together with those of a like mind. A truly corporate life means that responsible, adult people do things together from the necessity of their faith and because they are bound to one another in faith and love.

It is this kind of church life which lay people need and are looking for, insofar as they are looking to the church for anything. The need for this kind of life is being felt throughout the church. Throughout the world there are a great number of experiments being made to find a more satisfying, because more demanding, way of life. We call them experiments, for those who initiate them know indeed that they must try something new and are not confident that what they try will succeed, but what they are doing, however hesitatingly, has become their way of life. They are not trying to find a new pattern so that when they have discovered it they may settle down to follow it. Insofar as they have discovered anything it is that their unending life of trying is the only pattern of a personal, adult, responsible, and corporate life. So in churches in Britain, in Europe, and in America, you will find congregations that are trying out new patterns of church life which allow people to get to know one another in a personal way, which encourage them to discuss the anxieties and concerns of their ordinary lives, and which do so in a way that helps them to make their personal decisions and take their personal actions responsibly, supported by the understanding of how others come to theirs. There is no means of counting how many congregations throughout the world church are making such experiments. No one, who has the privilege of moving outside his own parish and of visiting and sharing the life of churches in other lands and of differing traditions from his own, can but be impressed by the variety and the seriousness and the success of these signs of life which challenge the old idea of an attentive, listening, and passive people and are intent on producing a responsible, active laity. The trouble is that so often each experimental group thinks that it is odd and alone. It has no idea that its aims and experiences are shared by innumerable other groups; that what it is doing represents a tide rising in the life of the church.

Because of this tendency for each group to see what it is doing as a trickle affecting one little area and not a flood that could fertilize all, it is well that a name has been given to one form in which this new experimental life has been expressed. The name of "house church" was first used by Ernest Southcott (now Provost of Southwark), when Vicar of Halton in Leeds, England, and it has been accepted as covering many experiments of this type. The advantage of this generic title is that it allows many different lines of action to be seen as widely similar. And the name itself — house church — emphasizes certain significant features of this attempt to find a more satisfying lay life in the church. It expresses the desire to break away from the domination of the ecclesiastical building. It emphasizes that the church is made up of people and that where they are there is the church. It suggests — and experience has borne this out — that if there are certain things that can be done adequately only in a building built for the purpose of worship, there are other things essential also for the Christian life that can be better done when men and women naturally gather.

Certainly they will discuss their own problems and concerns more feely in their homes than in the church hall. Decisions taken at a meeting in a house are seen as decisions they have taken and which they themselves must carry out and not, as often happens in the church building, what the officials of the church will carry out.

This urgent task of finding an adult, responsible pattern for the corporate life of a congregation depends for its fulfillment on the laity. It is indeed often the minister who alone can set the experiment going. The members of the church have been trained to depend on the vision and the impetus of the clergy. But these experiments cease to be experiments only when the laity who share in them know them to express the way of life they want to live in the church. In the end it is only the laity who can make them work and can allow them to develop into a full adult congregational life to replace our present infantile one. This task demands the vision and perseverance of a large number of lay people. It depends, in the end, on the emergence of a new kind of church member.

In the life of his local church the layman has a positive, radical, and indeed, revolutionary role to play. For this he will need training.

8. *The Layman's Leisure*

A few Christians have always been fortunate enough to have some spare time, and some indeed a good deal of spare income, after they have met the basic needs of their families and themselves. A book should be written about the way in which the antislavery movement, the campaign against child labor in factories, and the missionary movement (to name only three examples) gained enormously because some upper- and middle-class Christians in the last two hundred years have used their lives and their incomes to good effect. They did not need to work for a living; but they worked exceedingly hard on religious and social problems of one kind or another. They were wealthy, and they used their wealth to very good purpose, enjoying a freedom from both secular employer and religious authorities that modern laymen can very rarely experience.

Other Christian laymen have been equally fortunate, and yet have wasted their fortunes and their days to little useful end. John Wesley had hard things to say about the leisured gentlemen of his day; and it is difficult for us to see how committed Christians could have quite so easily joined in the extraordinary luxuries and privileges of the spacious days before 1914.

But all this is two wars ago; and the position in our so-called affluent society is entirely different. A few great fortunes remain, and quite a number of people inherit enough wealth never to have to work for a living. But the wonderful new fact about leisure is that it is now a practical possibility for millions and millions of ordinary people, who work something like a forty-hour week, enjoy two or three weeks' vacation with pay and a "long" weekend from Friday night to Monday morning, and maybe retire at sixty-five with fifteen years more to live. As Dr. J. C. Hoekendijk, of the University of Utrecht, wrote in *Laity* in September, 1961: "The new life will be less industrial than any we have experienced since the industrial revolution. . . . True, it is rather annoying, but much of what we have recently discovered about the place and task of the Church in industrial society will have to be discarded." Increasingly, too, these same people find that their real wages do increase. It is true that after meeting the basic needs of family life, despite all the increases in prices from time to time, they have more and more money to spare for semiluxuries and holidays. This is part of the tremendous social revolution which we are in the middle of, and it is not easy for us to understand how great the change is — until we talk to some of the working people who can still remember the days before 1914. The first "cost of living" index, prepared by the British Board of Trade in 1900, did not even include butter or electricity (as these were not considered part of any normal working-class budget); the latest, prepared in 1962, makes allowances for washing machines and TV sets.

Of course nobody must forget the senior citizens who share inadequately in this transformation of working-class life. Of course Christians must remind "prosperity" politicians of the slums still remaining, of the sizable pockets of unemployed, of the vast areas of the world where this revolution has only just started. And, of course, when everybody does achieve the living standards of New Canaan or of Beverly Hills, there will be plenty of problems left for man to face. But let it be said bluntly: very many people now have far more chances to buy the things and find the spare-time activities that help to make up a good and satisfying life, and Christians ought to rejoice that this is so. There is so often a depressing air of vague Puritanism (falsely so called) about Christian pronouncements on modern life.

The extent to which the Christian life is still thought of by so many people as purely a negative and prohibitionist thing is well illustrated by a report that came in May, 1962, from the Detroit Industrial Mission. Two members of their staff, James Campbell and Jesse Christman, wrote that to the majority of industrial workers in the city: "The Church means not swearing, smoking, drinking. It means hushing up sex, it often means forsaking union membership. It means avoiding associating with the 'unsaved.'"

And in January of the same year Dr. H. A. Hamilton, then chairman of the Congregational Union of England and Wales, wrote in *Christian Comment*: "A Christian to-day is a person who knows how to *choose*. He can live in a world of abundance and not be bewildered by it. In his use of time and money he reveals himself as a man whose values are never determined by the desire to keep up with his neighbours or to have the latest things on the market. He knows how to abound, as well as how to abase." Church people ought to be glad that many homes—particularly working-class homes in our grimy cities—are so much more comfortable than they used to be. And they ought to be very careful, in view of the reputation which they have for being censorious, before they condemn the way in which modern families spend their spare time and their spare money.

In particular, Christians must be more careful than they often are to distinguish between moral judgments and matters of taste. Nothing is more infuriating to a young layman than to have older Christians condemn his expert liking for jazz while they will approve heartily of Bach or Mozart (or, even worse, they will confuse jazz with pop music). Church people tend to be an elderly and traditionalist lot; they must be careful to let their Christian charity triumph over their instinctive dislike of new styles in clothes, music, art, and leisure-time activities. Indeed, we would suggest that after due allowance has been made for voluntary Christian service and voluntary Christian giving (to which we will return later in this chapter) the best rule is the famous saying by Augustine — in one of his brighter moments — Love God and do what you like!

"Love God and do what you like." We almost feel that it would be well to leave it at that; for Christians have such a reputation for mealymouthed advice to other people on how to spend their spare time "profitably," and how to avoid most of the ordinary pleasures of mankind. If, nevertheless, we venture to suggest certain ways in which laymen may all the more enjoy their spare time and their spare money — and give glory to God in doing so — we do this with real hesitation, and with an intention to avoid, as far as possible, offering rules and regulations that might cramp the freedom of a Christian man to order his own life under God.

Our suggestions may be conveniently though rather pompously grouped under two words: *consideration* and *discrimination.* It follows automatically from the Christian's duty to "love his neighbor" that he must show some consideration for the people he comes up against in shops, cafés, buses, and trains. It is fun occasionally to be waited on (especially if you are the kind of employee — or kind of housewife — who normally does the waiting). It is perfectly legitimate to use some spare money to purchase "service" of different kinds: we may hope that in an affluent society waiters and cooks themselves get enough wages to enjoy a week or two as customers. But it is *not* legitimate for Christian people to treat "servants" of any kind like dirt, even if they are unsatisfactory in their service. The same thing applies to the other people we all meet on our overcrowded beaches and our very overcrowded highways: it is not easy to love our neighbors on the Exeter bypass or the Pennsylvania Turnpike, especially when it is still pouring rain and the trip has been a doubtful success — but there is no discharge from this duty, all the waking days of our life; and some of the sourness of some modern vacations would be avoided if we simply remembered this. In a way weekends and evenings off are sometimes a rather childish attempt to "have it all our own way, for once" — this is the one thing which Christians may not ask for — and which no man will achieve anyway.

That is surely enough about *consideration,* which many British and American people still manage to show as a permanent and admirable habit of life. Perhaps we may say rather more about *discrimination* — which may be rather more attractively described as the art of making *choices* in life, as how you spend your money and how you spend your time.

We have said above, and we mean it, that Christians have to learn to be very tolerant about other people's choices. In particular, it is too easy to identify "right" choices with suburban "good taste" or with cultural fashions. Nevertheless, it is impossible to deny that many people find it difficult to spend their money and their time profitably and *enjoyably.* And Christians ought to be able to say as much, and learn the art of discrimination, and help their neighbors to do this, without becoming "snobs" of one kind or another. There is nothing commendable in being duped, in finding that you have wasted your money on a shoddy suite of furniture or a most unsatisfying vacation; and young Christians, in particular, need help in all this.

Two things have made this a more urgent matter than formerly. In the first place, many people from working-class backgrounds are enjoying incomes and moving into the kinds of jobs and homes which their parents and grandparents would have thought it wrong ever to dream about. They are becoming more and more "middle class." And many of the things which they may wish to spend money on are increasingly complicated and increasingly difficult to test in the shops — and also increasingly sold by cunning advertising that will deliberately discourage them from objective assessment of the goods or services on sale. It is not difficult to test the quality of some cookies — and in any case, if they are moldy you won't go back to that shop again, and at the worst you have lost a quarter. It is extremely difficult to test the quality and durability of a new house, or of a TV set, or of a secondhand car — and in each case there is a good deal of your "spare" money involved.

We have said in this book some rather hard things about middle-class church people and middle-class suburbs. But here is something in which the middle classes have really something to teach the world — the art of spending money wisely and enjoyably. It would be most valuable if Christians could work out ways in which this art and skill could be spread more widely abroad. The consumer magazines like *Which?* and *Consumer Reports* are most valuable — and are now bought by more than the inner core of traditional middle-class homes. Schools could do much more, and educational TV could perhaps do most of all. It is most important that Christian people should pull their weight in all this.

Our middle-class traditions have, too, something to say about the enjoyment of our spare time. It is not just cant to say that an active vacation may be more enjoyable than a purely passive one; and since working people now get more than a few hours each weekend, and more than a day or two for an annual vacation, it is significant that after the first few blissful hours of doing "absolutely nothing," the common complaint is one of being *bored.* It is excellent to see how many people spend their leisure hours "doing it themselves," how many are learning to fish, sail, and travel — above all travel about in their cars or their station wagons. Probably many more ought to be encouraged to do the same, so that the beautiful theories of educationalists and social workers about everybody having hobbies, or outdoor pursuits, or both, may at last be realized. (The figures for participation in such activities in the United States are already staggering.)

This chance of vacations, which are more than a blessed rest from heavy toil, is of great importance to Christians as individuals, as members of families, and as members of a community together. People are now getting great pleasure, not merely in going on vacation, but in planning it months ahead (starting immediately after Christmas, to judge from the torrent of press advertisements). They are prepared to put a sizable proportion of their annual budget into one major trip — and maybe a number of "long weekends" as well. Church people have not, however, properly worked out the implications of these theories. If everybody, and not just a chosen few, are to go on their travels, there will result a considerable invasion of quiet resorts and even good fishing rivers. There is already a wild variety of English accents in Scottish fishing pubs in August. If people are to have an active weekend, what happens to local church life on summer Sundays? (The German Church has a traveling church touring the trailer sites on Sunday mornings.) And what happens about Sunday observance, anyway? At a discussion in Widnes, Lancashire, not long ago, there was the usual attack on "godless" Sunday driving. It seemed necessary to point out that whereas all the participants in the discussion group lived in suburban roads with pleasant gardens to sit in on a hot Sunday afternoon, most of the families of Widnes had to put up with considerably less attractive housing. Were they really to be blamed if they used their cars and vans to seek the beauties of the Cheshire countryside across the River Mersey?

It seems indeed likely that discrimination is increasingly common when people choose where they go for weekends and holidays. We would dare to add a brief word about discrimination in cultural matters. Let us insist again that the church has little right to be censorious over light entertainment. Nevertheless, Christians cannot, in all conscience, be happy about an affluent family that spends almost all its time listening to pop music or watching TV Westerns. The point is not that these are "wrong," but that they are second-rate; and that it is the experience of very many people that much great enjoyment can be found, after a bit of trial and error, in jazz, in Beethoven, in a first-class film or play. If only lay training specialists can avoid the negative attitudes of so many Christian people over this! If only they could say, more often: "Yes, the Beatles are fun, and a TV Western is fun. But there are more riches to come. Try them occasionally, and remember life does not end at twenty-five — nor should your zest for trying something new!"

The careful reader will have noted, with a slight smile, that we threatened earlier in this chapter to say something about voluntary Christian service and voluntary Christian giving. Some writers on the duties of the layman would have talked about these matters much earlier in the chapter; indeed, they might have talked about little else. We have left them until the end quite deliberately, not because they are unimportant, but because, in our judgment, they are too often considered out of the general perspective of a Christian's routine of life.

Voluntary Christian service, in organizations such as Church World Service, church youth groups, or the Telephone Samaritans, is an extremely important part of the work of the church, and a necessary element in the life of almost any Christian. It is, however, normally more important for a man to run his office properly, sell in his store energetically and yet honestly, or see to his patients conscientiously, than it is for him to perform these duties in a mediocre way and then as it were "compensate" for this by flinging himself into "church" work. We rather suspect the story about the Baptist missionary Carey who is said to have dismissed his craft as a bootmaker rather contemptuously, claiming that his real aim in life was to "save souls." (It is to be hoped that his customers found their soles satisfactorily seen to as well.) It is also a doubtful gain in Christian living when a local church worker is so often out at "meetings" that he neglects his wife and family.

In the same way, the voluntary giving of considerable sums to church work or to other charities does *not* excuse the gaining of a fortune by doubtful means, or the management of most of one's income in a sloppy or extravagant or slightly dishonest way. The temptation to whitewash one's financial past by donations to hospitals or bequests to some kind of charitable foundation or other has of course been ludicrously evident in the lives of some American millionaires (and the church may indeed be profoundly thankful for this fashion in massive bequests to charity, helped on as they have been by generous tax exemptions). There are far more less wealthy Christians who have tended to put on one side, say 5 percent of their wealth, which they give away with considerable care as their "gift" to God, and forget that they are also responsible to him for the other 95 percent. Christian stewardship is about the whole 100 percent of our possessions, not one percent of which is ours absolutely.

It remains true that voluntary Christian service and voluntary Christian giving are basic to the organization and the work of the Christian church. We have two principles to suggest for lay people to argue about.

In the first place, we would urge very strongly that all churches and all Christians should ask constantly: How much of our voluntary work and how much of our voluntary giving goes to serve the *world?* How much is really just keeping the "club" going? There is sometimes a real tension here. We are not at all arguing that the basic essentials of a local church machinery should be neglected, like the minister's salary, the telephone bill, the payment of adequate (not stingy) remuneration for necessary full-time help. On the contrary, we would urge that the proper provision of these essentials is one of the prerequisites of any Christian organization — as they are for any human organization. Continental and American churches are far more sensible about this than their British counterparts. But the provision of essentials often goes on to the provision of many other things, which are not so clearly necessary — and the very success of different schemes of "planned giving" makes this a real temptation to a comfortable suburban church. Sometimes a "Christian stewardship" campaign may benefit most of all the comfort of the church members and the suppliers of church furniture and stained-glass windows! Indeed, some cynics have argued that Christian people give less to the outside world than they used to do — since they channel their giving more and more through the official church machinery, which does *not* pass it on to the world outside. The Rt. Rev. Trevor Huddleston, Bishop of Masasi in Tanganyika, had some sharp words to say about this at the 1963 annual rally of the Universities' Mission to Central Africa. He commented: "The Church of England is to-day giving to the whole Church overseas only five per cent of her total expenditure. This is less than half of what we gave fifty years ago. At the very moment when stewardship campaigns and the like are increasing the total income of the parishes in this rich country, African and Asian Christians presumably are considered to need less than before."

Bishop Huddleston referred to the proposal to rebuild one London church for five hundred thousand dollars (St. John's, Smith Square, which has been derelict for many years), and added: "This amount would permit me to build a permanent church and put a priest in every parish in my diocese. It would allow me to run my diocese for seven years without fear."

There should be more comments of this kind. For instance, it is a pity that the recent decision to spend no less than thirty thousand dollars on a new pulpit for St. Paul's Cathedral, London, was not more widely discussed.

The same thing may be said of much voluntary church work. To produce a church concert or dramatic play is a pleasant thing to do together, and there is nothing whatever wrong in Christians enjoying themselves in social functions of this kind. But this cannot count as *service* — as costly and sacrificial work for the outsider — unless, of course, the function concerned will be a piece of dramatic evangelism or teaching of some kind, or unless the cast includes some newcomers to the district, or some social misfits, or somebody from right outside the congregation. And it is rather too easy to enjoy a winter spent on a light opera and kid oneself that this is a vital Christian duty, because at the end of it all there is a hundred dollars more for the new church organ.

Even a good deal of the "necessary" church maintenance could be dispensed with if there were any economic utilization of church machinery and plant. There is a great waste of both clerical and lay manpower in keeping redundant churches going; there is a great waste of headquarters staff because so often the denominations insist on doing separately what they could perfectly well do together. Let there be a crisis in Lower Bongoland, and within six months there will be published in Britain seven or eight rather amateurish pamphlets on the subject from different church headquarters and missionary societies, in addition to those from the British Council of Churches (which, in theory, is supposed to do this kind of thing for the churches). Let there be a new and allegedly sinful dance for teen-agers, and five or six youth departments will organize a conference, a consultation, and/or a commission on the Wriggle and Juvenile Delinquency. One of the most sinful, yes sinful, results of disunity in the church, both between the denominations and within the denominations, is the sheer wicked economic waste of God's resources which it entails.

The second principle we would suggest for voluntary work and voluntary giving is that of "spreading the load." Many of the strains of family life and vocational loyalties that afflict a few Christian laymen occur because they are so few, because about 5 percent of the laity — the same people all the time — are called upon for voluntary work. (And often enough, as we have said in Chapters 4 and 5, these are the very people whom the church must send *out,* out into the unions or the Parent Teacher Associations, out into the front line of Christian service to the world.) We have in Britain only some 10 percent at most of the population whom we can expect to undertake regular church duties; but we have a very large number more of "fringe" people who would be prepared to lend a helping hand if they were asked. The church is pathetically unable to mobilize a large number of these people for social service, particularly if they are men or young people with technical and social skills, rather than with an academic education. And yet the educational psychologists have told us for fifty years that it is *doing things together* that produces "fellowship," that activity together is better than years of listening passively to sermons and instruction. Many of these people are willing to serve, the Christian church is an organization committed to service; and yet somehow all they are asked to do is to listen to sermons, sing incomprehensible hymns pitched far too high for comfort, and teach in Sunday school. At the same time, the few "really first-class" lay Christians are rushed off their feet keeping the machine going.

When it comes to voluntary giving, many churches have made admirable progress in recent years in persuading the majority of their members to contribute to maintenance and to benevolent funds. This is excellent, and means that many local churches are at last on a sound financial footing.

We would, however, venture to raise a gentle query about one aspect of "planned giving." It is entirely right that a local church should budget properly for its maintenance, and levy some kind of "membership fee" for its congregation; it is highly desirable that the same congregation should together plan some of its giving to people outside the congregation, to Church World Service, an overseas mission, and so on — and should raise this benevolence money efficiently together. But it is perhaps not wise for a Christian man or a Christian family entirely to leave their scheme of giving to a church committee or a regular plan. This is rather too safe a way of settling with one's conscience. We have been impressed with what a family may do together, if it decides to save even a modest sum together for some specific project, and *if it argues out together how to achieve this saving* — not by moving over to loincloths and an exclusively potato diet, but by contracting out of some of the more expensive fashions in keeping up with the Joneses. A good deal of the fun — yes, the fun — of Christian giving can be lost if everything is left to a church scheme.

9. *Training the Layman for His Work in the World*

We pointed out in Chapter 1 that most of God's people (which we called laity type "A") must work out their Christian obedience in their Monday to Saturday lives and their secular callings; only a minority (laity type "B") find their chief Christian duties in "church" work for a local parish or a national religious organization. The importance of adequate training for type "A" cannot be overemphasized, yet it has always been neglected by the church. Indeed, Dr. J. H. Oldham, the veteran Christian layman and founder of the Christian Frontier Council, gave it as his considered opinion in an important article in *Frontier* (Spring 1963) that "the new movements which have concerned themselves with the place of the laity in the Church have tended to confuse two entirely distinct problems. They are not wholly unrelated to one another, but they are quite different in character. The one is the question of the participation of the laity in the activities of the Church as an institution in society; . . . the second, quite different question, is how the layman can best serve the christian cause within the field of his own secular vocation."

Dr. Oldham adds: "When the leadership and initiative are in the hands of the clergy, it is psychologically almost inevitable that there should be a strong bias towards the things that they know about, and a deflection from questions which they know next to nothing about in first-hand experience. It is only in groups in which the lay element . . . predominates, and in which the clergy, if they participate at all, do so as learners and not as leaders, that the real problems of the layman in his daily occupation come to the fore."

Yet laity type "A" are the frontline troops of God's armies; these are the men and women who have to keep the faith and to survive in the gray world of business negotiations, labor union loyalties, local government contracts, party caucuses, popular journalism, competitive television, and the like. Their nurture and their support should be the first concern of the church.

This is true both for management people, and also for ordinary shopworkers and typists. The art of responsible compromise is something which both have to learn. As we saw in Chapter 4, *when* to stick your neck out, *when* to offer your resignation, when to wait patiently because the time has not yet come — we are so unskillful in all this kind of dilemma, and the church has offered us so little help.

The first thing to do is to try to use the ordinary apparatus of Christian education for the training of such laymen. There has been a tendency among some leaders in the continental lay movements to sweep aside all the traditional network of Christian education; and in the United States there have been some rugged pioneers who have condemned all the vast structure of church education there as beyond redemption. We hold strongly that this is too pessimistic a view. Much can be done with Sunday school lessons, men's groups, religious instruction in secondary schools (legally *compulsory* in Britain!), and the like. Admittedly, Christian educationalists, like all educationalists, tend to be conservative people — and often reflect in their little textbooks and their syllabi nineteenth-century views on the laity as on much else. But denominational leaders are often far ahead of local congregations and their pastors in understanding the problems of the laity; they can be wise and extremely influential allies if we will have the patience to penetrate to the relevant committees and offices at church headquarters. It is of the greatest importance that the people who direct Christian education departments, who run summer camps, who offer courses for youth leaders, shall reflect both in their lecturing and in their whole attitude toward the church the importance of the laity's work in the world. Otherwise there will be (some say there is) such a massive bias toward clericalization and churchiness that all the prophetic little pamphlets way out beyond the fringe of the institutional church will never correct it.

We would assert, then, that it is important to do what we can with the traditional structures of Christian education. Nevertheless, one of the most important developments in the lay movement in Europe since 1945 has been the beginnings of quite new methods of lay training, and the establishment of a whole network of new lay centers—which are still not very much understood in Britain or the States.

It is not possible to give a full account of this extraordinary development here, and reference should be made to the considerable amount of literature now available on the subject. It is quite remarkable that in at least four countries these lay centers, or "academies" as they are sometimes called, sprang up spontaneously at the end of the Second World War. In Germany, Dr. Eberhard Müller, formerly secretary of the German Student Christian Movement, established a center at the shabby spa of Bad Boll, near Stuttgart. He managed, incredibly enough, to have his first conferences for lawyers and journalists in the autumn of 1945: the Academy at Bad Boll now has a staff of nearly 150 and a tremendous calendar of conferences for lay people throughout the year. Other areas of Germany followed, and there are now some thirty-eight lay centers grouped together in a German Association of Academy

Directors — which in 1961 reached a total of about 10,000 people with their conferences.

In Britain, William Temple College, in Rugby, established in 1944 in memory of the great layman's archbishop, became in 1945 a center for industrial lay work under the skillful direction of Miss Mollie Batten, herself a senior civil servant. From the start Dr. George MacLeod intended the Iona Community in Scotland to be an experiment in partnership between young parsons and industrial workers; other lay training work on the island has developed into an annual program of lectures and youth camps, and there is a network of Iona lay associates of different kinds.

In Switzerland a group of individuals headed by an educator, Dr. Hans-Jacob Rinderknecht, established a center at Boldern-Männedorf, near Zurich. And in the Netherlands a group of men carried out plans which they had prepared in a Nazi concentration camp and established the famous center of Kerk en Wereld (The Church and the World) at Driebergen, near Utrecht. These centers and many more are now grouped together in the Association of Directors of European Lay Centers; and church leaders all over North America and in Asia, Africa, and the Caribbean are planning similar centers for their own areas.

What, briefly, are the particular advantages of these lay centers? What, indeed, do they do more than any diocesan conference house or holiday center?

In the first place, they hold to the principle that they call Dialogue. By this they mean that an academy is not a place for preaching at the world, nor lecturing it, nor brainwashing it, nor even subtly conditioning it to religious ways of thinking. It is a place for dialogue, for discussion, for hammering out together the problems of life today. This process may take place between different kinds of Christians, between pastors and lay people, and above all, between Christians and non-Christians, between different races and classes, between conservatives and radicals, between East and West. And these discussions are not rigged so that always there is a neat Christian answer given during the closing minutes; it is frequently said in academy circles that the church must learn to listen as well as to speak, and in particular the expert on a given topic is readily and respectfully heard, whether he is a confessing Christian or not.

Dr. Kathleen Bliss has urged strongly in her paperback *We the People* that this ought to be a principle for all church education: "Teaching in the Church ought to take the form in which the laity have to stand up for their faith in the world, that is, in dialogue. The laity are aware that their explanations often fail to convince, that they are countered by questions they cannot answer, that situations arise in the world to which faith seems irrelevant, that much of the personal morality taught in the Church cannot be translated straight into the situations of group responsibility, decision and action which predominate in considerable areas of life. They have to grapple with problems of family breakdown, young people going adrift, illness, death, crisis and boredom. All this must be said within the teaching life of the congregation."

This principle of Dialogue is complemented by a second principle which we may call Integrity. These non-Christian experts would never go near an academy but for the absolute assurance, guaranteed in advance, that neither they nor their listeners would be "got at." Of course these lay training centers are Christian centers, openly and avowedly; but people who visit there are, as a matter of principle, given that human freedom of thought and speech which our Lord himself respected. There is no attempt to hustle people, willy-nilly, into the Kingdom or to "convert" them by dubious psychological or emotional group pressures.

It is one of the great gifts of God to our times that in Germany, in particular, such centers of Christian citizenship and social concern should have flourished—and also that so quickly after the last war Germans, Dutch, French, and British lay leaders should have developed together these new techniques of lay training. It is in Germany, too, that a second great experiment in lay training has developed—the Kirchentag, or German Layman's Congress.

Here again we can only mention this movement briefly. Some of the features of the Kirchentag have perhaps been dismissed rather too lightly by foreign observers: a meeting that brings together not only 400,000 people for a giant rally but (far more important) 40,000 people for *four days* of Christian instruction and fellowship is a new phenomenon in Christian history. And the various experiments on similar lines in other countries, such as the Rassemblements in France, the Kirk Weeks in Scotland, and the Kerk Dagen in Holland, show that the combination of a mass rally and a conference is not merely something that Germans can manage. The different elements of a Kirchentag are worth analyzing briefly.

In the first place, a Kirchentag must reflect the true doctrine of the laity, or it is useless. The great value of the German Kirchentag, ever since the first was held in ruined Essen in 1950, is that it has always called the German laity to a lively and responsible life in the world, that it has dared to argue about controversial topics of world politics, of German unity, of labor union organization, of the times of Hitler and of Khrushchev. (It is entirely typical that the most important section of the Kirchentag in Berlin, in 1961, in the year of the Eichmann trial, was entitled "Jews and Christians." Prominent Jewish speakers shared the platform with Christians throughout.)

In the second place, a Kirchentag attempts to become something of a national event. When a German Kirchentag opens, the bells ring in every Protestant church in Germany; when it closes, the TV network accepts an hour's program. There are enough people around to stop the traffic. Indeed the town, receiving 40,000 visitors for most of a week and 400,000 on the Sunday, definitely knows that a Kirchentag is on! (There is an admirable tradition by which Roman Catholic families take in Protestant visitors to the Kirchentag; in return, Protestants are asked to offer hospitality to Catholics during a Katholikentag. The Cardinal Archbishop of Munich himself entertained a Danish Lutheran bishop who was a special delegate to the Kirchentag in Munich in 1959.) It is normal for the President of the German Federal Republic to attend the final rally of a Kirchentag, and other leaders in both state and church recognize this as a very major national event. This is worth noting—it is perhaps a pity that the major religious functions in Britain which Authority attends in state are coronations, State funerals, and the General Assembly of the Church of Scotland.

Thirdly, and this is important, a Kirchentag must represent a mastery of the most modern techniques of mass meetings, transport, and organization. As Dr. von Thadden has pointed out, the twentieth century has given us new chances of coming together in large numbers; it is right that we should use them. We would add that a Kirchentag that was badly organized, badly publicized, with poor loudspeakers and inadequate refreshments, would be a damnable thing to experience. But a Kirchentag that goes well is a wonderful experience: there is a symbolic importance (especially for nonintellectual people) in big gatherings together, and this needs to be emphasized. Many a lonely Christian is surprised to find how many of God's army there may be giving up a week of their annual vacation to be together for instruction and refreshment.

Of course there is one clear danger in meetings of 400,000 people together. The whole thing can become too passive, even too regimented. It needs to be emphasized that neither the great German Kirchentag nor the smaller ones elsewhere have shown the slightest danger of becoming military demonstrations like the Nuremberg party rallies of the Nazi days; a Kirchentag crowd is much more like a London coronation crowd than a military demonstration. On the other hand, everyone connected with the German Kirchentag will admit the dangers of merely passively listening to the meetings; it is very difficult to do anything else when you are hearing distinguished speakers through loudspeakers together with five thousand other people. Nevertheless, there are developing most strenuous efforts to break down the whole membership of a Kirchentag into smaller discussion groups — for some years now the thousand or more foreign visitors have been offered small groups in a special Ecumenical Center, and for the Dortmund Kirchentag in 1963 a massive attempt was made to divide up the German participants as well. One of the most interesting developments in the smaller Swiss, French, and Scottish Kirchentags has been the emphasis on small-group discussions.

It is probably fair to say that special extraparochial methods are particularly needed in the training of Christians engaged in management, in the professions, and in similarly "responsible" positions. This is simply because most normal congregations never have enough doctors, or advertising specialists, or labor union officials to provide such people with a group for discussion and fellowship together. In many parts of Canada and the United States, in Britain and on the Continent, such people are more and more developing informal groups or associations to discuss their common problems. In Europe, it is very often a lay center that offers them a base for their activities.

Such groups are often suspect to church authorities (and sometimes sit pretty lightly to denominational disciplines). It does seem, though, that they are a valuable new form of lay training and discussion, and that certain principles are important if they are to flourish.

In the first place, such professional groups should normally be interdenominational. The success of the Christian Frontier Council in London, England (one of the first of these groups, founded by Dr. J. H. Oldham in 1939), is very considerably due to the fact that members of all churches, including Roman Catholics, have been able to join it. There is a dreadful tendency to restrict professional groups to one denomination: surely we should be spared the appalling prospect of Societies of Anglican Dentists or Associations of Lutheran Schoolteachers!

But in the second place, such discussion groups, though they may fairly claim to be part of the whole church of Christ trying together to find his will in their professional callings, cannot be and must not try to be a substitute for the normal institutional church — split though it is into irritating denominations, and organized though it often is in unattractive patterns of local church life. It may well be that some of the "fringe" members of a professional group will not be — and for the time being should not be — regularly asked to be communicant members of a Christian denomination. But if the ordinary members of such a group neglect their ordinary local churches, they may become nothing more than a cultured religious huddle together (and in any case, what happens to the other members of their families?).

On the other hand, denominational church authorities ought to restrain their natural impulses to interfere with, to denominationalize, to keep a protective hand over, all these spontaneous groups. They ought to accept the need for *multiple loyalties,* by which a man will recognize some obligation to his local church (maybe not quite all that the local minister will hope for), and in addition a loyalty to a monthly meeting, say, of his Christian society or group of some kind or another. The whole body of Christ is not just a local church, nor just one denomination — nor is it just a group of Christians arguing until two in the morning about the H-bomb.

In all this training of the laity for their work in the world the shortage is one of teachers — of people competent to suggest to young businessmen or shop stewards or merchants lines on which they may work out their daily Christian obedience. And these teachers must be for the most part *senior laity* who have survived in their chosen occupation — both as Christians and as human beings. It is a senior Christian real estate agent who can support, encourage, and help a junior Christian realtor; it is a teacher who has kept sane and healthy and cheerful for twenty years — and still calls himself a Christian — who can help a young "dedicated" Christian novice at the game; it is a veteran Christian labor unionist, who has fought both Communist enthusiasm and non-Communist apathy all his life, who can put new fire into the belly of a young Christian worker, disillusioned after his first year or two in the factory. These senior, worldly, battered, often very tired laity may surely claim to know something of the mind of Christ for their particular calling and daily routine.

We may suggest, incidentally, that it is an excellent thing that not only educated lay people (as we said in Chapter 5) but also clergy can try to specialize in one secular discipline, as well as in theology. The number of people who can relate theology to psychology, theology to sociology, theology to business economics, are pitifully few. A minister who has a good mind, and a really stern self-discipline so that he does some reading after he leaves seminary, can help a lot here — but we suggest that he will need to *specialize,* to narrow his serious reading to one vocational field, if he is ever to be sufficiently well-informed to speak with authority to the lay experts in that field. There are not enough clergy in the coalfields who know really well, better than most mining engineers, the problems of the coal industry. There are not enough clergy who have really mastered the history and the economics of the oil industry, the intricate problems of the urban renewal of Glasgow or of Boston, the social problems of the West Indies or of Appalachia. If they will read enough, and *listen* enough, then they can help Christian lay people who are caught up in these industries and areas. But if they offer easy generalizations, they will be listened to politely, and dismissed as easily.

These senior laity who must bear the main burden of training their juniors are always very busy people. They must nevertheless be expected to help with this training, *and this should be recognized as their main Christian duty and their main function in the Church.* They are all too often persuaded to undertake minor parish duties. They are conscientious people; and they agree to be church treasurers or delegates to the synod, or to help with the annual dramatic production. This can be very bad indeed; for this sometimes means that they neglect their secular duties in the employers' association, the union, or the neighborhood. And in any case, their first duty is not to prop up the local institutional church, but to pass on their scarce skill, their all too rare professional knowledge — how to be a Christian layman in their particular occupation. Local clergy must learn to deny themselves some of their best lay help, and remember that in any secular organization, the most scarce skills are most carefully used — you do not put patternmakers on general maintenance work.

This will be a hard saying for some parishes — which are appallingly short of any laity — especially lay*men* — to help their overworked parsons. Who can blame a clergyman in a downtown area for seizing eagerly at the few good Christian veterans he can find — the artisan, the foreman, the local doctor or teacher — and urging them as their simple Christian duty that they must help him to "keep the parish alive"? Yet here, we dare to suggest, is the crucial point at which the priorities must be kept right, the point at which the parish may have to lose its soul to save it, and allow these men to move into lay training groups of their own where they can train other laymen in their daily responsibilities.

Of course many senior laity will at once reply: "All very well, but we have never been trained to be articulate about our daily lives. We know how to be church treasurers, and to sing in the choir. We don't really know how to be Christian advertising executives or tax accountants. We muddle through, somehow; but we wouldn't exactly like to say how — and we certainly wouldn't like to set ourselves up as examples to our juniors!"

We have already made some reference to this attitude of diffidence in Chapter 4, and we have suggested that in a way this is a kind of craving after a false perfectionism, no more to be found in accountants than in parish ministers. But when such senior laity say that they don't know *how* to undertake such informal education of their juniors, they certainly have a point. There is a great need in our churches for something like the advanced courses of some of the German academies, almost something like a Christian staff college for advanced lay training.

Here again the time factor soon enters in. When on earth are senior laymen to find the time to study the theological implications of their faith and the ways in which they may establish and pass on some kind of professional Christian tradition of lay obedience in their particular jobs? We would only suggest here that they should decide carefully how much time they can give to this kind of work for the Lord, and then divide it fifty-fifty. For instance, a very busy personnel manager might decide that if he is not to neglect his responsibilities to his firm and his family and his professional association, then all he would be able to offer to the church would be two weekends a year. Then he should try to spend one of these weekends arguing out with his equals what his Christian duties and responsibilities are as a personnel manager, and the other weekend offering to speak at a conference of some group where junior executives will be ready to learn something from him (and of course, argue with him, too — there is very little of the "Listen to me, I'm the expert and know the answers" attitude in this kind of lay training). And the church — both his denominational authorities and his local pastor — should be satisfied to have these two weekends, and have them used in this way, and not in some parish function.

It may very well be that some of these advanced discussion groups should be organized not only interdenominationally but also nationally — or even internationally. We are not convinced that the annual crop of Christian conferences is yet sufficiently well organized or specialized to meet the needs of expert laymen, though some of the meetings at William Temple College, in Rugby, at some of the lay colleges in Holland and in Germany, and at the World Council of Churches Institute at Bossey, near Geneva, really go deep enough into the problems on the agenda for lay people there to feel that they are getting beyond pious generalizations. Other laymen's conferences that we have suffered are a shocking waste of travel money and of time — which is almost more important when one considers the long journeys, sometimes from the ends of the earth, which are involved. It is of the first importance that in this age of conferences the whole world church learns to be careful and efficient in its demands on the scanty spare time and scanty travel funds which its lay people can command.

We would venture to emphasize in conclusion one element in the training of the laity for their work in the world which we regard as of particular importance, and yet one which has been much neglected in the life of the church until recent years. The training of the laity proceeds not merely by exhortation, instruction, and discussion, but by the conscious or unconscious attitudes achieved over the years in the *worship* of the local church. It is of course true that when a local congregation is gathered together to worship Almighty God, there are very many more things to be emphasized besides the daily duties of Christian people. Nevertheless, this worship must, in some way, by reference or by omission, show *some* attitude of the church to the layman's daily responsibilities; and it can be argued that almost all fashions of worship in the church today still show a wrong one!

Some of the experiments in house churches are important here, and in particular some of those made by members of the Iona Community. For instance, when George Wilkie, now Industrial Organizer for the Church of Scotland, wrote in *Christian Comment* for January, 1962, about the house churches in his former parish of Port Glasgow, he said: "Another need which the House Church seems to answer is the opportunity for relevant and effective service for others. . . . The House Church gives an opportunity for spontaneous neighbourly service in the most natural way." And the "order for service" for a typical house meeting in Port Glasgow is as follows:

Prayer.
Bible Study.
Roll Call. We go over the list of members, and arrange for help for anyone in need.
Service of the Neighborhood. "Anyone in need in this or that street?" It is seldom that there is no one.
Tea, biscuits, and chatter. Perhaps discussion of some subject of national or local concern.
Home-going prayers. Real intercession of the parish goes on in these prayers, for the people we have been talking about.

In more normal styles of worship it is rare to find any adequate recognition of the *partnership* between clergy and laity which should now prevail. This is no matter of churchmanship: some very "protestant" local churches leave the congregation as passive participants in the service, and some churches which lay great stress on sacramental worship emphasize strongly that the whole body of Christ is concerned with each Communion. But even in a parish Eucharist, there is not often much explicit reference to what has been called Saturday night and Monday morning life — even the intercessions or "biddings" may have little reference to local life, or to Christians involved in local strikes or elections or welfare work. The hymns so often reflect a "pie in the sky when you die if you have been sufficiently pious" outlook. And of course the whole range of Christian symbolism, coming to us from a long past agricultural age, must increasingly be scrutinized as to its relevance to the layman's life today.

It is interesting that some of the art for the new Coventry Cathedral has been criticized for precisely this point. Of course, clergy who have been trained in this kind of specialist knowledge can perhaps manage to "translate" all these things into modern theological insights — just as a specialist in sixteenth-century language can see wondrous things in Marlowe — but to what extent can they expect that an electronics engineer or a supermarket manager must necessarily learn their technical jargon before he understands what God will have him do on Monday morning? We overstate the case, because we are not convinced that all the talk about a revision of the liturgy, especially in the Church of England, has come to much from the point of view of the worldly layman. We may even suggest that *The New English Bible* tends to be written in *Times* English rather than in timeless English.

10. *Training the Layman for His Work in the Local Church*

It will have been clear from the contents of Chapter 7 that the subject of this chapter *is* of fundamental importance, even though some of the emphasis of this book is on keeping many lay people rather more off church premises. Partly because of the shortage of clergy and ministers, "churchy" laity are now essential to the running of many church services and organizations — the Methodist Church in England has always relied on them, and on a typical Sunday some 60 percent of its pulpits will be occupied by lay people. Both the Methodist Conference and the General Assembly of the Church of Scotland include something like 50 percent lay people. Even the Church of England is now trying to "use" its laity more and more, and casting a perplexed eye on the Scottish "eldership." In the United States, the position of leading lay people is often crucial in determining, for example, the attitude of a local church toward Negroes.

The question of training the laity for such church responsibilities is much discussed nowadays (when indeed, some church leaders and writers regrettably fall into the major error of assuming that this is *all* that lay training involves). In many parts of the world, particularly in the States, church "lay training" centers and institutes and courses are becoming the fashion.

It is fortunately true that this interest in training the layman in his church responsibilities and duties has already produced interesting and important results. In the United States many of the branches of men's work and women's work have gone far beyond a weekly social meeting, and now undertake thorough training in the responsibilities of church membership. The different American schemes of "stewardship" and "planned giving," whatever their faults, do produce an extraordinary amount of money for religious and social work overseas, besides financing the greatest wave of church-building that Christians have seen for many centuries. In England the same kind of stewardship campaign, or every member canvass, has made very many lay people, especially men, much more active in their church membership than they ever were before; and Anglican bishops are now vying with one another to open diocesan lay training centers for their further education. In Scotland there is a new emphasis on the eldership and on training for this high office. We have the impression that British Methodists are not content to point to the vast numbers of local preachers and lay officials, without whom their church could not last for a single Sunday, but that they are anxious as never before to improve the quality of their training and of their service for God. And there seems no end to the calendar of conferences for the laity, either in Britain or in America, nor any limit to the instruction that they will faithfully imbibe.

All this means that there is less need to deal extensively with such training here. We would, however, venture to suggest that some of these schemes and courses get rather into a rut: both their content and their techniques of informal education may need looking at. In particular, we would insist that lay people undertaking work with their local church or with their church bureaucracy need, quite as much as anybody else, to be grounded in the fundamental doctrine of the laity. They too must accept that it is the first duty of the church to exist for the people outside it; and they must not allow themselves in any way to regard themselves as "superior" to fellow Christians working out their Christian loyalties off church premises. And they must, in very practical terms, learn to cooperate as partners with the parsons. This is much easier to accept as a theory than to work out in practice in a traditional church atmosphere, where for many years the minister has expected and has been expected to take the lead in everything—and to be the spiritual expert in everything too. As we have seen, in many parishes it is the "churchy" laity who prove the greatest handicap to the parson as he tries to teach the true doctrine of the whole people of God. They so often expect him always to lead the meeting, to take the chair, and to decide "spiritual" matters by some kind of divine right.

Church laity often need, and to their credit often ask for, more thorough instruction in the faith. Can we be entirely happy about many of the schemes which have been produced to meet these requests? So often they seem a kind of watered-down theological college course, full of technical jargon which requires quite a high level of literary education to appreciate, and insufficiently relevant to life in the twentieth century. Should not a critical eye be cast over many of the books of theology written for laymen, and even more some of the pamphlets, textbooks, and magazines offered to Sunday school teachers? It is not much use having an occasional TV program or conference speech or magazine article about the true doctrine of the laity if a false doctrine is taught or implied in many of the usual teaching magazines and techniques of the church! We have noted in Chapter 9 that there is a certain tendency among the leaders of the lay movement, especially in Germany and in the States, to assume that the ordinary church apparatus of Christian education is so corrupt as to be beyond redemption: such an attitude seems foolish enough, but the penetration of this educational network (quite as conservative as most secular educational networks tend to be) is a tricky and exhausting process. How much of the true doctrine of the laity is reflected in those little books given to young people at confirmation, or the millions of parish magazines circulated in Britain?

It is extremely important that those members of the church who find their chief Christian duties on church premises must be trained and encouraged to keep their contacts with the outside world. Like the parson, and perhaps even more than he, they have the temptation to consider themselves the "holy few," and to develop an excessively puritan and narrow-minded attitude to the world which God made for us to enjoy. Indeed some denominations may even demand of them (by custom if not by church law) a particularly puritan way of life with regard to drinking, dancing, and other normal entertainments. These laity will be recognized in the district as being "real church people" as (unfortunately) their fellow Christians on the city council or golf club committee may not be. What kind of impression of Christ's church will they give? They will be extremely busy people and this is probably inevitable in the present state of the institutional church in many areas. *They must, at all costs, be encouraged to have at least one nonchurch engagement each week.*

One aspect of the work and training of the "churchy" laity needs special attention from our church employers: it has been more thoroughly and profitably studied on the Continent and in the United States. Not only at the local level but at national church headquarters a good many lay people are now "professional Christians." They are employed full-time in keeping the church structure going. For this work, we lack in Britain adequate theological insights and adequate tests of efficiency. There is still a certain amount of quiet sneering about any attempt to run the church efficiently; this attitude is a hangover from the days when the church (like much else) was run in a rather slovenly fashion by gentlemen of leisure. It is also profoundly wrong from the point of view of any proper doctrine of Creation; not only woods and beasts and streams are meant to be used for God's glory, but also telephones, typewriters, office lighting, and skillful typography. The church of God should use every piece of human knowledge it can, and this includes the skills of office administration and accounting. "Heaven on the Hudson," the multistory Interchurch Center at 475 Riverside Drive, New York, used by the National Council of the Churches of Christ in the U.S.A. and other religious bodies, is often laughed at by British visitors to the States. Yet is our miscellaneous collection of British church premises really preferable?

Even more serious is the extraordinary way in which some church bodies, from national headquarters down to local churches, exploit their lay employees. It is part of the freedom of a Christian man or woman to decide to lead a sacrificial life, to work extra hard, to give away most of his income in one way or another, prayerfully decided. It is impertinent of church bodies to decide that their employees shall lead compulsorily sacrificial and deprived lives, by paying them badly, or offering them contemptible pensions. Such workers, especially if they are women, are too often "too good to complain" — let some of the worldly laity complain for them! Of course lavishness is out of place in church administration, of course church people should use modest hotels, and economical transport, and be careful about building up office staffs à la Parkinson; but any worldly expert on administration will tell you what you lose by not giving executive personnel adequate equipment and assistance.

11. *Training the Parson to Work with the Layman*

The recovery of the laity means the recovery of the church. When the members of the church in their life together know what it means to be in Christ and when they see what this life commits them to in their work in the world, they will begin to know what the church is, and so will men outside. This would be a recovery of the relevance of the gospel for the world and undoubtedly it is only by the obedience of ordinary Christian men that this recovery can be made. It would be a recovery of something long lost to sight, but for the church as we know it — or, to be more honest, for ourselves — it would be discovery rather than recovery. This unfreezing of the frozen assets of the church would be for us like the discovery of a new continent or a new element.

It is not too much to use such language of the discovery that laymen have to make and alone can make. For the layman to find that he is called and enabled to take up a life of responsible action in the world is to penetrate a new continent, terrifying and exhilarating. To find that the Christian life is no longer to be lived at second hand, to realize that he is the pioneer of the faith in the new world of today is to discover a new element in life, and one for which he has had no training.

In this chapter we want to deal with the part of the clergy in this and, in particular, with the training of the clergy in its relation to this task. This is not just to bring in something in the end which cannot be ignored. This chapter is by no means an appendix. It deals with a question that is quite fundamental. The training of the laity cannot be divorced from the work of the clergy. The training of the clergy cannot ignore the work of the laity. The theological education of the ministry can no longer be regarded as a purely professional matter. It is crucial to the ministry of the laity.

Theological education has become the whipping boy for all the ills of the church. Perhaps there is more justification than we often think for attributing the cause of our ills to the nature of our present theological education — for reasons which will be discussed below. We have not begun seriously to question and discuss the nature and purpose of our theological education. We have accepted the pattern and been content to discuss the logical adequacy of the curriculum. We have not seriously studied its effect on its students or its effectiveness in the life of the church. Nor have we adequately formulated its purpose in the life of the church today.

In this chapter we shall be critical of the seminary training given to the clergy. What is said is based partly on the experience of the Iona Community during the twenty-five years of its existence. This experience has of course been limited, but it has been constant and fairly intimate. The Iona Community each year recruits into its full membership young men who have just completed their education in seminary and who are at the outset of their ministry. Though an integral part of the Church of Scotland, it has in its full membership those of other churches — Episcopalian, Methodist, Congregational, Baptist — as well as men from Presbyterian churches in other countries, and particularly the U.S.A. It thus welcomes men from a variety of theological backgrounds. They stay on Iona for the first three months of their training, sharing life with those engaged in the work of rebuilding and, indeed, for half the time doing manual work under them. The Iona

Community has thus an almost unique opportunity to study the end product of theological education, in conditions that test the ordinand's ability to work and communicate with laymen.

Certain impressions grow with the years.

The first is that these men were much freer in their relations with other men and much more able to communicate with them before they entered seminary than afterward.

The second impression is that, despite the greater attention given in theological seminaries to professional training, the gap between the studies of the seminaries and the work of the church to which the students go is too wide for some of them to jump. The desire to postpone the jump by undertaking postgraduate studies becomes very great. It may well be that much of the trouble lies in the inadequacy of the work of the local church. This does not lessen the gap or excuse the failure of the seminaries to train their men to make the jump.

The third impression is of the very strong but quite distinct way of thinking that each seminary imposes on its students. The seminaries seem to want to produce conformists and not experimenters.

The fourth and final impression is of the depressing effect of theological education on those who endure it. Some come out of seminary disillusioned and in despair. Others come out seeking any other work than that of the ordinary parish ministry.

But quite apart from these criticisms of the training of the parson, there are two main reasons why the question of theological education is crucial for the laity.

The first reason is that the whole new idea of the work and therefore of the training of the laity represents a shift from the conception of a church that is minister-centered to that of a church that is primarily concerned with the life and witness of its members. The training of the clergy which the denominations have developed is aimed at training men to serve a minister-centered church—and is indeed training them to be the managers, the key men, or, in the words of Bishop Lesslie Newbigin, the "prima donnas" of the church.

A church that sees the service of its members in the world as its main witness brings to the clergy a new idea of their tasks. It is as inevitable as it is right that the clergy, being the trained, full-time servants of the church, should be involved in the training of the laity. But the acceptance of the training of the laity as the primary job of the church, and of the training of the clergy as secondary to it, demands a difficult reorientation in their thinking. Perhaps more ministers than laymen have indeed made this reorientation in their thinking and are attempting to put it into practice. But they are not helped by their training.

The second reason why this question of theological training is so crucial to the ministry of the laity is that the theological education of the clergy has in the last hundred years come to acquire a dominant and determining place in the life of the churches, unknown before. It is as difficult for us to think of the church without theological seminaries as it is for us to think of the church of the first centuries without ecclesiastical buildings. Today in the churches of the West a tremendous deal of time, thought, and money is devoted to the development of a large apparatus, housed in many buildings and employing a large and carefully chosen staff, specifically to train men for the ministry of the church. The church has accepted this as necessary for efficiency. But it has done more. It has given its seminaries such authority that they now occupy a formative and determinative position in the church. This means that any change in the life of the church is hard to achieve unless it first finds a place in theological education.

The surprising thing is that this whole accepted structure of theological education has been built up, in Britain at least, only in the last hundred years. Of course there has always been theological education in the church. But it was only in the 1840's that specialized seminaries for the professional training of the clergy began to be set up, at least so far as the national churches of England and Scotland are concerned. There have been a hundred Archbishops of Canterbury, but only three were trained in a seminary. The rest, including so recent an Archbishop as William Temple and indeed the present Archbishop of Canterbury, got on without this experience and seemingly got on quite well. Seminaries are now so accepted as an essential part of the organization of the church that it is important to remember how recent a development they represent and to assess how they have affected the mission of the church and, in particular, the ministry of the laity.

It is important, however, to remember that these Presbyterian and Anglican colleges of the 1840's were not the first in Britain. The earliest colleges for the training of men for the ministry were opened by the independent churches in England in the eighteenth century, when the universities were closed to dissenters. But because of this their colleges were never merely professional schools for the training of the ministry. They had to provide a general education and were not confined to students studying for the ministry.

It is also important to remember that the true pioneers of the specialist theological college are to be found in America. The United States was by decades the pioneer of theological education in specialist colleges even as it was the pioneer, by more decades, of university education for women. Pittsburgh Theological Seminary was founded in 1794; Princeton Theological Seminary in 1812; Yale Divinity School in 1822; Lutheran (Gettysburg) Theological Seminary in 1826; Union Theological Seminary, New York, in 1836.

Before the forties of the last century the intending minister of the Church of England or of the Church of Scotland took his chance with his contemporaries in getting what would have been called "a gentleman's education" at the university — or elsewhere. If he were of the Church of England, he went to Oxford or Cambridge. If he were of the Church of Scotland, he went to one of the four Scottish universities. In these universities there were indeed professors of divinity, of Hebrew, and of church history. There were classes that he could attend, as he attended classes in moral and natural philosophy and mathematics. But there was no separate college for theological students. There was nothing in the way of practical training. There was, of course, the religious life of the university, but this they shared with all other students. The training that the intending minister received was in the life of his family, of his parish church, and of the general community. If he received any specific training for his work, it was under the tutelage of a parish minister with whom he lived for a time. This was true of both churches.

This sharing of a common life and education with contemporaries who intended entering other professions was a vital part of the education of the clergy. The clergyman was never extracted from this common life. He was not a specialist. His education with other people and his experience in sharing the life of the parish made him the "person" (parson) of the place and gave him a position that was social and magisterial rather than religious. Eighteenth-century biographies and novels are clear witness to this sharing of a common life and this social position in England and in Scotland. We see this reflected in the same century in America. In an address at the 150th anniversary of the opening of Princeton Theological Seminary, Dr. Robert F. Goheen, president of Princeton University, reminded us that in earlier days: "Prospective magistrates and ministers studied together, which was perhaps difficult and good for both. And eloquent still is the prayer for Princeton University voiced by Gilbert Tennent in 1757: that she might be 'a diffuse and durable blessing, for Church and State, for all future time.' "

This meant not only that ministers had read the same books as their educated lay contemporaries, but also that the training of Episcopalians and Presbyterians was not greatly different. Whether a man was an Englishman or a Scot, an Episcopalian or a Presbyterian, his education was much the same. The lives of English clergymen and of Scottish ministers, at least of those sufficiently eminent to gain biographies up to the first half of the last century, show the same pattern — some years at a university, followed by travel abroad as tutor to a wealthy youth, or a year of teaching in school or college, and then, at a very early age, into a parish on the nomination of a patron. It shocks us by the inadequacy of the training, but it meant at least that ministers of differing churches could talk not only with their own people but with one another. They were not divided by their training.

This centuries-old pattern began to be changed before the middle of the last century. In providing a specialized, professional training for their ministers, the Protestant churches could be said to be departing from the teaching of the Reformers and favoring the new practices of the Roman Church of the Counter-Reformation. Luther and Calvin emphasized the need of education for all young people and saw the education for the ministry as part of the provision of "a sound general education of youth for the service of the State." The Roman Church, on the other hand, soon after the Reformation set up separate colleges for the training of its clergy.

In Scotland the founding of theological seminaries for the training of ministers was due to division in the church and not to any new ideas about the training of the clergy. So long as the professors of divinity in the Scottish universities were ministers of the Established Church, the churches that drew together those who had seceded felt the necessity of founding their own college to educate their own ministers. But it was with the Disruption of 1843, which drew off half the ministers and members of the Church of Scotland to form the Free Church, that the Scottish theological seminaries which we now know came into existence. New College in Edinburgh was founded in 1846; the college in Aberdeen now called Christ's College was founded in 1847. The college in Glasgow, now called Trinity College, was founded in 1855. So little was the idea of a reform of theological education in the minds of those who set up these colleges that their aim could be described as the creation of a replica of the teaching of the universities, and indeed at the start there was the hint of a hope of founding not another theological faculty but a rival university. These new seminaries sought to carry on the educational tradition of the post-Reformation centuries. They provided instruction in theology, church history, and the original texts of the Bible. The spiritual discipline of the students was not in the hands of the college but in the hands of the church. So there was no need for a college chapel. There was also no department of practical training. These facts may seem strange to us today. But they do not indicate a disregard for devotional discipline or for the work of the ministry. They, rather, witness to the Reformation belief that discipline belonged to the courts of the church and prayer had its right place in family and public worship.

The establishment of these seminaries and the consequent separation of theological students from their fellows brought inevitable changes. Separation brought a greater concentration on theology. The fact that the foundation of these seminaries arose out of a tragic division in the church meant that there was a strong denominational emphasis in the teaching and life of the seminaries. The fact that all the students were training for the ministry of one church encouraged a new professionalism which had its good and its bad sides. All these inevitably led to the raising in the seminaries of questions of discipline and worship — to the founding of departments of practical training and the improvising of chapels — and to the development of a kind of life in the seminaries very different from the intention of the founders.

Church of England seminaries came into existence a little later. St. Bees was founded in 1816, Chichester in 1839, Wells in 1840, St. Aidan's in 1847. They owed their existence to causes very different from that which led to the founding of the Scottish seminaries. They arose not so much out of division in the Church of England as out of a new concern for the training of the clergy. This was due in the main to a new self-consciousness in the Church of England and to a realization of its task in the changed conditions of mid-nineteenth-century England. The old non-professional method of educating the clergy seemed to many to be inadequate, especially after reforms had been made in the Universities of Oxford and Cambridge, by which church control was loosened, Fellows of college need no longer be ordained, and teaching became more secular. At the same time many in the church were aware of the new and difficult tasks that the industrial revolution had brought, especially in the cities. And if there was no split in the church, as in Scotland, to necessitate the foundation of separate theological seminaries, there were new parties in the Church of England who were anxious to see that men were trained according to their views. So the Anglican seminaries were started usually as party seminaries, dedicated to a particular church policy. But, despite their theological differences, they shared a common pattern, diametrically opposed to the pattern of the Scottish seminaries of the time. The Anglican seminaries were founded deliberately to train men for the practical work of the parish and were concerned above all things with the development of the life of prayer and devotional discipline in the men themselves. For this reason they were residential. The Scots seminary was based on the eighteenth-century university. The Anglican seminary was modeled on the monastery.

The founding and maintenance during the last hundred years of seminaries by all the churches represents a development in the use of the churches' resources, a radically new conception of the training needed for the clergy, and the deploying of some of the ablest men in the church into this task of training. Our debt to this new conception of ministerial training would be hard to evaluate. It is certainly very great. First, there has been the development of theological and particularly Biblical studies. It is doubtful if the understanding of the Bible which modern scholarship has brought would ever have penetrated to the ministry of the church and therefore, to some extent, to the members, if it had not been for the seminaries. It would have remained the exclusive possession of the universities. Then there is probably little doubt that the training given in the seminaries has produced a more efficient and a more dedicated ministry. Thirdly, but with less certainty, it may well be that were it not for the seminaries the churches would be faced with a more serious problem of recruiting men for the ministry than at present.

The gains to the church can hardly be exaggerated. But we have also to count the cost that has been paid. It is not small. It can be put under three heads.

The first and, perhaps, the heaviest cost has been in the accentuation of denominational differences. The seminaries in Britain have been founded by denominations or by parties inside a denomination. They have owed their existence either to a split in a church or to the emergence of conflicting opinions in a church. In America this denominational emphasis of the earlier colleges has been balanced by union or undenominational theological seminaries. And this means of overcoming denominational interests through a common theological training has been followed by the younger churches in Africa and Asia. It has not yet found favor in Britain, where theological education still bears witness to a divided church. The cliché is often heard today that the minister of the local church of any denomination represents the universal church among people who cannot but be parochial and denominational, just as the foreign missionary is said to do. Undoubtedly many ministers feel the call to be this, but in obeying it, they are fighting against the whole of their training. It could more logically be argued that the ordinary members of the church in their ignorance more truly represent the one universal church and by their ignorance protest against the denominationalism of their minister.

Even more powerful as a cause of division than the denominational foundation of the seminaries has been the divergence of the lines of training that they have followed. This has been particularly obvious in the difference between the Episcopalian seminaries based on the monastic pattern of the medieval convent and the Presbyterian seminaries founded on the pattern of a post-Reformation university. What we are concerned with here is not the relative value or even the relative out-of-dateness of the two models but the effect of their difference in leading the churches they serve out of the range of conversation. Whereas till the beginning of the last century the ministers of the Churches of England and Scotland could talk together because they had read the same books and had the background of the same kind of life in home and parish and university, now what divides them as much as anything is the religous language that they have learned in their seminaries. It divides them from one another. It also divides them from ordinary men. This is a very heavy price for the church to pay.

The second price that has been paid has been in the detachment of the clergy from the ordinary life of the people. When we read the eighteenth-century diary of an English vicar such as Woodforde or when we read Galt's *Annals of the Parish,* which, though in the form of fiction, gives a good picture of a Scottish rural parish, we see how much at home the parish minister, in England and in Scotland, was in the life of his people. He had his part in the secular affairs of his rural parish because he worked his glebe and fulfilled his duties as a magistrate. This pattern of life has not survived and the minister would have had in any case to find a new relationship to his people. But it was a tragedy that when a new and different kind of life began to develop with rapidity and unforeseen problems arose in the new industrial areas, the churches should decide to take their intending ministers away from a life shared with their contemporaries and shut them up in specialist seminaries, often far removed geographically and always far removed mentally from the life of the new industrial centers of population. The words of Thomas Chalmers at the laying of the foundation stone of New College in Edinburgh in 1846 are significant: "We leave to others the passions and problems of this world, and nothing will ever be taught, I trust, in any of our Halls, which shall have the remotest tendency to disturb the existing order of things, or to confound the ranks and distinctions which now obtain in Society."

The original purpose of the theological seminaries was not directed toward an understanding of what was happening economically and socially in the life of the country, nor toward training men for a new kind of ministry in new conditions. It was directed toward sustaining a kind of life in the church which was already out of touch with events. The life of faith that the colleges tried to develop among their students was based either on a medieval monastic pattern or on the social life of a rural parish. It is no wonder that the church still sees the preindustrial rural parish as the ideal pattern and that the language of its worship sounds medieval in the ears of modern men.

Probably nothing has done more to cut off the church in Britain from the life of industrial men than the foundation of theological seminaries. But responsibility lay in the theology that was behind their foundation and that inspired their development. There is no proof that all would have been well without the seminaries. In Germany, for instance, where theological education remained within the universities and theological students all through their course rub shoulders with their secular contemporaries, there has been an even greater isolation of the church from the life of industry. We may attribute this to the length of the theological course and the fact that students enter it from high school and are therefore never anything but theological students, and even more, to the isolation of theology from other studies. The church in Britain, with a different experience of education and with the chance of being pioneers in the approach to the problems of modern industrial life, might have chosen another line. It might at least have set up the new seminaries in industrial areas. Efforts are now being made to repair the damage, by experiments of training ordinands through living in industrial areas and sharing the life of men in industry. But the price that has been paid is heavy.

The third price paid has been in the damage done to the image of the laity by the new professionalism of the clergy. In the old days the minister was the "person" (parson) of the place. His authority and influence were due largely to the fact that he belonged to the parish and had no professional interests. It was the fact that he was not a specialist that made what he did and said in the name of the church and its Head something that the people knew that he did with and for them.

The aim of the new theological education was to make

him a professional. The purpose of the theological seminary is to train men to serve the church efficiently. What the late Prof. Richard Niebuhr, of Yale, said of American theological seminaries is true also of British seminaries: "Their express purpose is to educate men who will direct the affairs of Church institutions, especially local churches." There is much to be said for the training of men to serve the church. It is, indeed, essential. No institution of the size and with the responsibility of the church could achieve much without a trained, full-time service. The church today, if it is adequately to witness to Christ in the new world in which we live, will need more and better trained servants than it has ever had in the past. The church will need these if the ordinary lay men and women of the church are to be enabled to do their job. The unfortunate thing is that the church has identified ordination with full-time professional service. The two are distinct and indeed opposite in their intention. The man who is ordained is ordained to represent or identify himself with the people. The man who is trained to a profession is trained to be different from them.

In the seminaries this identification of ordination and professional service became complete and accepted. Their foundation left no place for the training of laymen in the service of the church. As the church felt the need for new and developing forms of service in the church, the church added more to the curriculum of the seminaries. And so it has gone on. The present emphasis on pastoral theology — on the study of pastoral psychology and on training in counseling — has its danger in implying not that this is the church's work but that it must be carried out by the ordained ministry. The church has not begun by asking what its members who are professionally trained are already doing in those fields but by asking how it can train its clergy to do something amateurishly in these fields. More and more the minister is seen as the one on whom the life and work of the church solely depends.

How can a professional training have any other effect? The cost has lain in denying any training to the laity and, indeed, any place for them of real service and leadership in the church. The seminaries have cut the ministry off from the laity by denying the laity any vital place in the work of the church and any particular training for their work in the world.

The situation is the more difficult in that what is needed is not a reformation of the seminaries, as if they were corrupt, or an elaboration of their curricula, as if they were inefficient, but a radical change of direction and an abandonment of their isolation. We have to face the fact that if there is no radical change in the training of the clergy the danger to the church will be some form of secession on the part of groups of the laity — or the slow or not so slow decline in active membership.

What is needed is, first of all, a recognition by clergy and laity alike that their membership in the church is common and shared equally by all. A minister should remember that his primary calling is in his baptism and not in his ordination. There is no hierarchy in the membership of the church, though there may be in its service.

This fundamental condition of the common membership of the church, shared by clergy and laity alike, needs to find expression in the life and worship of the church — all the more urgently when so much of our present practice emphasizes differences of status. The formal words of our worship state clearly that we have all sinned and are all forgiven; our visible practice contradicts this. Means of demonstrating our fundamental common membership in Christ must be found. In one parish in Scotland the practice is to hold each year a service for the renewing of vows. The service begins with the common renewal of the vows taken by all at Baptism and confirmation. This is followed by the renewing of the vows taken by elders at their ordination. Then a member of the congregation reminds the minister of the vows he took at his ordination and at his induction to the parish; and he renews them. This service is of great value in itself in reminding everyone of the vows that they have taken. It is of special importance because it sets the vows of the minister in their proper setting, after the vows of the people in which he has joined as a member. The demonstration of this is of vital importance both to the minister and to the people.

This simple recognition that he is a layman before he is a minister and that he remains a layman while he is a minister — if by "layman" we mean, as we must, simply a member of the church, one of the people of God — implies a new attitude to the church. When the emphasis begins to be put on the ministry of the whole people of the church, the minister is forced into a new attitude toward his own job. The training of the whole people acquires primary importance. His peculiar ministry is to serve this. It is to this end that he undergoes special training.

How is the church to train men for this task? How is the church to ensure that the training it must give its clergy helps them to forward and not retard the training of the laity? How, in particular, is the church to overcome the faults of the present system which has increased denominationalism, cut off the clergy from an understanding of industrial life, and imposed a false professionalism on them to the distortion of the whole life of the church?

Any kind of training involves some separation of those being trained, and inevitably and rightly results in codes of behavior which are professional. This professional separation does not affect only ordinands. In medicine, law, the sciences, and education we find the same thing. These faculties are increasingly aware that the separation deemed necessary for professional training can be bought at too heavy a price. Their place inside the greater life of a university is cherished, just because it challenges this and at the same time offers the opportunity of conversation between those whose interest in a subject is professional and those whose interests are quite different.

If the isolation necessary for specialization is a handicap in the training of doctors and lawyers and teachers, it is much more of a handicap in the training of ministers and theologians. All specialist studies touch on human life. Medicine may be beyond the understanding of the common man, but what it studies — health and disease — is his concern and no one else's. Law is a highly specialized study, but it is the people, through their representatives, who make the law and not the lawyers. In an even more fundamental way the material of theology is the common affair of men. The minister or the theologian can never be a professional in the sense in which a surgeon or a lawyer or a plumber is. If I break my leg, I am wise not to try to deal with it myself. I would be wise to put myself unquestioningly in the hands of a doctor. It is prudent not to be one's own lawyer. If a pipe bursts in my house, it is best to call a plumber and keep out of his way. But with religion it is an entirely different matter. The essential job of a minister is not to do something for me but to help me to do something myself: not to pray for me but to help me to pray, not to worship in my name but to help me to offer my worship with the worship of the church. As a member of the church, I am not a patient or a client or one whose absence will help things most. The unique things that the minister does in the name of the church, such as celebrating the Sacraments, he does with me and other men. In it I have my part to play. This is of course also true to a degree of other professions: especially is it true of medicine and education. The doctor helps me to regain my health. The teacher assists me to learn. The similarity should not surprise us. It should rather help us to realize how much more it is true of the work of the parson and of the theologian.

The peculiar job of the parson is in the interpretation

and edification of experience common to all who share the faith. He is ordained to the ministry of Word and Sacrament, to communication and communion, to deal with what unites and not with what divides men. The unique function that the church calls him to fulfill, the things that he alone is ordained to do, he never does alone. He does these in the name of the church, and not in his own name. Even more, he needs the participation of other persons if he is to do them at all. The celebration of the Sacraments demands the participation of the laity. The ministry of the Word is not the right of uninterrupted utterance from a pulpit but the duty of seeing that the Word has free course among men. The minister is ordained not that he alone may talk but that others may hear and understand and act. The experience and understanding of the laity are as essential to the fulfilling of the ministry of the Word as the theological education of the clergy.

The job of a parson is thus, essentially, for men and women and with them. The name "parson" expresses this identification, as we have seen. The name "minister" emphasizes the relationship of service. His training must be to this end. It must be seen not as something that separates him from other men. It helps, perhaps, to realize that even today he shares already most of his basic theological education with other men. No man's theological education begins when he enters seminary. His basic theological education has begun long before that — in his home, his local church, his school, his apprenticeship or university. All education is basically theological in that it inculcates a view of the world and of life. A man's theological education has been going on all the time from his birth. It comes permanently and enlighteningly through the life he shares with others and especially from the unofficial teachers he chooses and the truths come to him unsought but not unexplained. When we discuss the training of the clergy, we have to take account of this, the basic education that men receive, with all its possibilities and all its obvious shortcomings. It is basic because it is shared with the laity and because it is the foundation of the common life of a people.

If the clergy's training is not rooted in this general education, which they share with the laity, the clergy will not be able to serve the laity or to assist in this training.

In this general education there is, of course, place for more specifically theological education. It is unfortunate if we think that the instruction of children has nothing to do with theology. We cannot escape teaching theology whenever we teach and whatever we teach. This is why it is so essential that the study of theology, in its widest sense, should find its place in the teaching of a university, not just as a preparation for ordinands or for those who wish to teach religion in schools.

But even if theology begins to be thought of not as being particularly and almost exclusively for the training of professional ministers, there is still need for the particular and professional training of those who are to be the full-time servants of the church. The argument of this chapter is that this is an urgent and inescapable problem for the church: that the function of the clergy requires a new definition, that the method of this training needs a revolutionary overhaul, and that the very content of the teaching of theology has to be revised. All this follows from the recognition that the present weakness of the church is due to the ineffectiveness of its members: that the church is made up of God's unemployed, most of whom don't worry to draw their spiritual dole, that nothing is likely to happen until the clergy learn to see their place in the emancipation of the laity.

Wherever movements have taken place in the emancipation of the laity, whenever laymen have begun to show curiosity, initiative and responsibility, the minister, who has probably been pleading for these things from the pulpit, finds himself in an odd position. He has been trained to be the one leader in the parish, to be responsible for everything, to tell others what to do and what to believe. If he is sincere in wishing to see lay leadership emerge in the church, he has to draw aside and not interfere too much and certainly he must not be dogmatic. Where there are local groups or "house churches" — and one Scottish parish has over fifty — he has to be content *not* to know everything they are thinking and doing. And when the members of the church begin through these means to get down to the discussion of their own problems, he finds that he is the layman — in the sense of being the uninformed, that he has to learn from them of the problems of living today.

In place of the active, responsible leadership for which he has been trained he has to help to train others to take responsibility. He has to encourage them to take action in areas of life which he can know only at second hand. The combination of this self-effacing service with the leadership of worship calls for peculiar qualities in men and for a very different kind of training from that commonly to be found in theological seminaries.

It is also essential that the clergy be trained in the knowledge of what the training of the laity involves and trained to find their peculiar place in that training. Too often today the training given to lay people is a watered-down and insipid version of the training of ministers. We don't want to see the mistake reversed and ordinands learning in a garbled way about the training of the laity. There would need to be a full and intelligent understanding on each side of what the other is doing. Perhaps one of the most useful ways would be to have laymen involved in the education of the clergy: not merely by coming in to give talks on various experiments in lay training but by having a layman of special qualification as a full and equal member of the teaching staff — to make sure that secular thinking has its impact on theological training and that those whom ordinands are being trained to serve should not be forgotten or misunderstood.

The world must be allowed to break into theological education. The world is part of the material of theology, for Christian theology is not merely about God but about the God who created the world and redeemed it in Jesus Christ. Quite apart from the expediency of training the servants of the church to speak the language of today and to understand the thinking of men today, there is needed the realization that the Christian faith means nothing unless it is an immediate thing — that the only knowledge of God that matters is a knowledge of God now, that the doctrines of creation and redemption are meaningless unless men believe, with fear and hope, that God is at work in this world and in all men now, and that to invoke the blessing of the Holy Spirit is to confess that we are called to immediate personal action in this world at this moment. From any personal confrontation of the modern world the seminaries have withdrawn the servants of Christ's church. Today, in many seminaries, attempts are being made to remedy this. This is done generally by making mention of some topical problem and by trying to understand how it affects the church and the work of the ministry. If the question is of the relevance of Christian doctrine, all that is often done is to show that Augustine or Aquinas or Luther or Calvin had perhaps something relevant to say. This is really to train men to escape from a decision by telling a story — and this sometimes seems to the exasperated layman to be the main purpose of theological education. Why is it that so often, in a book or a course of lectures on some general topic such as war or justice or forgiveness, or on some controversial issue such as marriage and divorce or the place of women in church and society, will be found a historical account of what the doctors of the church or the councils of the church have taught in the past, told intelligently and carefully, but either stopping when the accepted textbooks cease to be helpful or ending with the most vague generalizations about present problems?

There will be no adequate training of the laity until the church in its most serious thinking begins to take the world in which we live as the area of its study in which it has to interpret the hand of God. This is the world in which the layman lives and works and in which he must witness and serve. It is also God's world, the only world of his that we know.

This painful confrontation of the world must find its outlet both in a new appreciation of the content of theology and in new experiments in clinical training. In many seminaries in Britain and America significant advances in clinical training have been made. These have been mainly in giving theological students practical insight into the treatment of psychiatric cases, into the work of the courts, and into casework. This is all to the good, but it is apt to bolster up the ideas that the minister is concerned only with the personal problems of individuals and that he is the only person in the church who can deal with them. This pastoral care of an individual is dealing only with bits of his life. Men and women have other problems: social and political problems; questions about their work; the appalling, and therefore often suppressed, questions about nuclear weapons and the possibility of a future for their children. In England an effort is being made to see that ordinands do have a personal experience of life in industry, and this leads to an awareness of the insistence of questions other than purely personal ones. Do many seminaries send their students to take part in political meetings and encourage them to serve in political parties — or to take part in demonstrations or strikes? Is not this a field of training as important as the psychiatrist's consulting room? There are, fortunately, some seminaries that work along these lines.

This experimentation in new ways of theological training in the present seminaries is important and is, probably, the main way in which exploration of more radical reforms will begin. But it will only be a tinkering with the problems unless there is the realization — or discovery — of two things. One, the lesser, is that the fundamental training on which the future of the church depends is the training of the laity and that the training of the clergy has to be seen as fitting into and serving this. The second and by far the more important thing is the realization that theology has to do with the whole church and the whole of life. In the days when theology was most creative, it was not the concern merely of the clergy nor was it seen as a matter exclusively of their professional training. It was a subject in which laymen and laywomen were engaged. It is as well to remember that Calvin was not ordained when he wrote his *Institutes.* In a day when the laity is educated and when the intellectual questions are set by the laymen — the scientist, the economist, and the politician — it is essential that theology be seen as the one subject to which all have to contribute, when the contribution of the secular specialist and the experience of the laity in their life and work in the world are of supreme importance. It is probably only when theology becomes concerned with the common life of men and with the urgent problems of the world's life that the denominational, professional seminary will become an anachronism. For then, indeed, there will be the beginning of a church that is one.

Then the clergy will find again the nature of their particular vocation. It is only when the laity becomes active in obedience that the ministry of Word and Sacrament is seen in its true meaning and has its full freedom of operation. When the ministry of every member of the church is recognized, then — and only then — will the limited and self-denying ministry of Word and Sacrament be seen to be truly the service of others and the service of Jesus Christ.

12. *Action Must Hurt*

It is not easy to end this book on an optimistic note. There is some chance that it may be read, and even discussed a little. There are many books "cooking" on the laity; and all this scribbling, and the fuss made about the laity at the New Delhi meetings of the World Council of Churches in November, 1961, and the present uneasiness about the position of the clergy may well together produce certain predictable results both in the United States and in Britain.

In the States the new emphasis on the laity is already approaching the proportions of a major trend in religious activity. Not only the National Council of Churches but increasingly the giant denominational headquarters are allocating staggering quotas of manpower and magnificent sums of money for lay training of one kind or another. Their annual programs are full of retreats, lay institutes, lay academies, lay summer schools, and the like. Indeed, some church leaders are mobilizing the laity at breakneck speed — and leading them into the church vestries. For the damnable thing about so much of this admirably efficient lay programming is that it is so much concerned with the duties of the layman in his local church, and so little concerned with his duties in the office and the plant and the supermarket and the downtown slum.

Some of the reasons for this frightening distortion of the true vocation of the laity are clear enough (and have already been implied in earlier chapters of this book). It is not only theologically disturbing, it is psychologically unnerving to try to work out your Christian duty as an AFL–CIO official, as a drugstore proprietor, as an advertising account executive. And if you try, the Church on First Avenue will often neither understand nor be able to help, nor will it be prepared to let you skip choir practice so you can have the time to think. It is as if army training for frontline service always took second place to preparation for formal parades and/or the unit concert — and a new wave of enthusiasm for a more efficient army simply meant *more and more time* spent on parades and concert rehearsals, so that recruits ended up by having even less time and opportunity for battle training.

In Britain, we do not have to fear quite the same lavish (though misguided) attention on lay training. Certainly not; for this would imply energetic planning, efficient financing, and a great deal of hard work — and all these qualities are now strangely suspect to us. (It must, somehow, have been different in the days of Wilberforce and Shaftesbury.) It is not the function of this book to analyze the present malaise of British industry and politics (though a lively laity would make for a lively national life, make no mistake about that). What is important here and now is to recognize that this malaise has affected God's church in Britain quite as much as any other of the older, soldier institutions in the country. Economists and sociologists have almost as much to teach us about the structure of the church as they have about the present state of our highways or the Clyde shipbuilding industry; and the two major evils of out-of-date capital equipment and inadequate leadership are as noticeable in, for example, the Church of England as they are in British Railways.

This means that in Britain any "lay movement" will take time to move — perhaps half a century or more, like our "new" network of highways (first planned in 1944) or our replacement plans for slum schools (first drafted around 1920). Indeed, it is to be feared that already the impact of some of our lay pioneers has been lost: Dr. J. H. Oldham, still at ninety-two years of age writing better stuff than his spiritual grandchildren, said in *Frontier* (March, 1962): "The questions to which we sought to find the answer in the Christian Frontier effort (founded in 1939) still remain largely without an answer. The first necessity is to recognize that this is so. It is scarcely even in any serious sense on the agenda, so to speak, of the Churches. An effort on the heroic scale is needed to reverse what appears to be the increasing tendency towards the church-centredness of the Christian witness in the world to-day. The need to make some really new beginning seems as urgent as it did twenty-five years ago — even, perhaps, more urgent."

But Christians have no right to sit down and weep; though we do have a duty to assess the position realistically, despite the protests of disloyalty and cynicism which may possibly follow from critics of our preceding paragraphs. This book is an attempt to talk about the work and place of the layman, and not, except by implication, about his devotional life. But for Christians to write anything about God's people without mentioning the Holy Spirit is like arranging a party without considering the Chief Guest, who will at once be the Reviver and the Entertainer of the whole gathering.

Now: it is fundamental to the New Testament that God does not send the wisdom and the power of his Spirit reluctantly, grudgingly, like a sour schoolmaster allowing only ten minutes off for a picnic. The only thing that stops this power and this wisdom from transforming God's laity is *ourselves,* both individually and in our family and our social groupings. We can cramp his style: we often do. That is why we must often be bitterly ashamed with ourselves for our petty status-seeking and comfort-loving and fairly blameless and largely useless private lives. That is why we must not only laugh at but also systematically wrestle with the dead weight of American religiosity and British slovenliness. There is much that we can do.

In the first place, we can examine ourselves. It is disturbing to reflect how "personal religion" has often decayed into negative sanctimoniousness or private scrupulosity; but let us admit frankly that the people that like to be called "conservative evangelicals" — Billy Graham types and the like — often achieve a personal discipline of life and a willingness to serve their neighbors (maybe in most unsuitable ways) which put more enlightened Christians to shame. It is very doubtful whether we shall ever learn our duty as laymen in the world, or show our neighbors anything of the love of God for them, without a great deal more hard work, late night traveling, dull social visiting, and duller local committees — and also more self-denial when it comes to status cars, expensive homes, lavish vacations, and so on. Heaven forbid that Christians should once again compete in being killjoys; and certainly in the Manchester or the Chicago climate it is unwise for us to go about in loincloths or live in tents. But we all, not just the clergy, need to watch the old temptation — that what the Joneses buy we need to buy too, so that we can "identify" with them (and no doubt understand their credit problems).

It is not only our financial and social habits that we must examine. We have to achieve a stewardship of *time* as well as of money. And our time is strictly limited. If you use time for engagement A you cannot have it for engagement B. If you spend a couple of hours on the church social, you cannot have those two hours for the local integrated housing committee or the Parent Teacher Association.

Such personal probing into our daily lives sounds almost unfair and unpleasant — as it is. Yet this may be the nub of the matter for many of us: our traditional patterns of spending and of week-night activities may be the very things that cramp our Lord's style, that stop the Holy Spirit from flooding into the set and stubborn patterns of our lives.

"But what's the use?" you mutter. "What can *I* do? I don't have the mainstream of the lay revival past my door;

and the church at the corner has broken better Christians than me."

You are quite right, and you are quite wrong. In the first place, even one or two spiritually strong individuals (who may by no means be "leader types" psychologically) can have a quite fantastic effect if they really put themselves at the disposal of God. It is not only that they may move mountains of local prejudice and suspicion. Even if they don't shift the mountains an inch, they very often inspire their children, and their friends, and their friends' children to greater things. In the second place, you should not be, and you will not be, alone for long. Nothing is more certain than that God intends his people to work in groups, in fellowships, together. All over the place, cutting across the whole messy entanglements of denominational barriers, there are springing up informal groups of Christians, clerical and lay together, who really care about God's world. You will find one, if you look hard. And these groups are genuine manifestations of God's church — they are indeed in some ways "house churches" together, and you can find fun and strength and wisdom in them. Of course these groups too (like, maybe, many of the original "Oxford Groups" and many of the "prayer fellowships" of our more pious students) can become corrupted into horrid holy huddles or coteries of religious beatniks, openly or secretly despising their struggling local churches. The test is simple: How much time do they spend serving the world — really serving the world, without religious scalp-hunting or theological patronizing?

In the third place, you may be lucky, and find not merely an *informal* group of lively, outward-looking Christians, but also a local church, even one of your own denomination, which spends as much time talking about the Christian in politics as it does about the Christian in the choir, and which centers its worship and its teaching on the love of God for his world — and not merely for his church.

There *are* such churches; and there are far more clergy aching to make such a transformation of their churches, no matter what the cost — but who are held back all the time by the conservatism of their laity. Those church leaders and local clergy who are prepared to pay the price for such a revolution — indeed such a "conversion" — in their churches are undoubtedly in a minority. But they are increasingly vocal, and they deserve every atom of support we can give them.

Nevertheless, we cannot avoid the cutting edge of the gospel — and indeed our great aim and longing in seeking a new vitality in God's laity is that we may find together a new sharp briskness in our faith, instead of the soggy platitudes which have lulled us to sleep. In a famous essay on "Holy Worldliness," Dr. Alec Vidler wrote: "Certainly there will be great risks in a Christianity of genuine worldliness, for it means living in the open air, it means living with men and serving them in all those areas where Christ is never named though they belong to him, or where he is named only to be misunderstood or reviled."

To be a real layman, in the second half of the twentieth century, is to undertake a hard and often uncertain pilgrimage. It is to struggle with a fog of ethical uncertainties, it is to face the misunderstanding of both friend and critic, it is to face accusations of being "disloyal," and "worldly," on the one hand — and yet on the other to be thought oddly scrupulous, something of a "sucker," someone to be exploited. And this is our true vocation. Perhaps Dr. Michael Ramsey, Archbishop of Canterbury, summed it up best in his sharp words to the 1963 Congress of the British Student Christian Movement, when he said to them: "Because there is in you the Glory, as our Lord's passion and resurrection have defined it, there will be in you a deep sensitivity, blended with a deep serenity. In your service of others you will feel, you will care, you will be hurt, you will have your heart broken. And it is doubtful if any of us can do anything at all until we have been very much hurt, and until our hearts have been very much broken. And that is because God's gift to us is the glory of Christ *crucified* — being really sensitive to the pain and sorrow that does exist in so much of the world.

"With this, a serenity that is deep in you — and because it's deep in you it brings to others peace and healing. 'Peace I leave with you. My peace I give unto you.' The life of a Christian ought to be like the ocean, with the surface constantly battered about by storms, but miles and miles below deep peace, unmoved tranquillity."

The layman has no right to try to avoid the storms.

takes untold years to really approach this depth
Unlimited time to get to this feeling

WRFD - 12:30 Talk back on sermons
after First Community.

Bibliography

This is not in any sense intended to be exhaustive. The World Council of Churches has already published a bibliography on the laity with over a thousand items. We simply offer a short list of basic books available in Britain and the United States (some of them quite stiff reading) and then some more popular books, pamphlets, and periodicals.

1. *Basic Books*

Bonhoeffer, Dietrich, *Prisoner for God* (title of British edition, *Letters and Papers from Prison*). The Macmillan Company, 1954.

Come, Arnold B., *Agents of Reconciliation* (Revised and Enlarged Edition). The Westminster Press, 1964.

Kraemer, Hendrik, *A Theology of the Laity*. The Westminster Press, 1959.

MacLeod, G. F., *Only One Way Left*. Iona Community, Glasgow, 1956.

Marty, Martin E., *Second Chance for American Protestants*. Harper & Row, Publishers, Inc., 1963.

Morton, T. Ralph, *Community of Faith*. Haddam House Book, Association Press, 1954.

Oldham, J. H., *Life Is Commitment*. Harper & Row, Publishers, Inc., 1953; abridged, paperback edition, Association Press, 1959.

Wickham, E. R. (Bishop of Middleton), *Church and People in an Industrial City*. Lutterworth Press, London, 1957.

Winter, Gibson, *The New Creation as Metropolis*. Doubleday & Company, Inc., 1963.

——— *The Suburban Captivity of the Churches.* Doubleday & Company, Inc., 1961.

2. *Other Material*

Ayres, Francis O., *The Ministry of the Laity.* The Westminster Press, 1962.

Berger, Peter L., *The Noise of Solemn Assemblies.* Doubleday & Company, Inc., 1961.

——— *The Precarious Vision.* Doubleday & Company, Inc., 1961.

Bliss, Kathleen, *We the People.* SCM Press, Ltd., London, 1963. A book about laity.

Casteel, John L., *Renewal in Retreats.* Association Press, 1959.

Frakes, Margaret, *Bridges to Understanding.* Muhlenberg Press, 1960. A book about European lay centers.

Gable, J. Lee, *Church and World Encounter.* United Church Press, 1964. The German Academies.

Gibbs, Mark, ed., *Meet the Church.* World Council of Churches, 1959. A booklet about the Kirchentag movement.

Hall, Cameron, ed., *On-the-Job Ethics.* National Council of Churches, 1963.

Hühne, Werner, *A Man to Be Reckoned With: Thadden Trieglaff and the German Kirchentag,* ed. by Mark Gibbs. SCM Press, Ltd., London, 1961.

Jenkins, Daniel, *Equality and Excellence.* SCM Press, Ltd., London, 1962.

Littell, Franklin H., *The German Phoenix: The Church in Post War Germany.* Doubleday & Company, Inc., 1960.

Michoneau, Abbé G., *Revolution in a City Parish.* The Newman Press, 1950.

Morton, T. Ralph, *The Iona Community Story.* Alec R. Allenson, Inc., 1957.

——— *The Twelve Together.* Iona Community, Glasgow, 1956.

Munby, D. L., *Christianity and Economic Problems.* St. Martin's Press, Inc., 1956.

——— *God and the Rich Society.* Oxford University Press, 1961.

Neill, Stephen, and Weber, Hans-Ruedi, eds., *The Layman in Christian History.* The Westminster Press, 1963.

Stringfellow, William, *My People Is the Enemy.* Holt, Rinehart and Winston, Inc., 1964.

——— *A Private and Public Faith.* Wm. B. Eerdmans Publishing Company, 1962.

Warren, M. A. C., *The Christian Imperative.* SCM Press, Ltd., London, 1955.

Webber, G. W., *The Congregation in Mission.* Abingdon Press, 1964.

Weber, Hans-Ruedi, ed., *Signs of Renewal.* World Council of Churches, 1957. A booklet about the Academy movement.

Younger, George D., *The Church and Urban Power Structure.* The Westminster Press, 1963.

We venture to mention certain periodicals with which we are involved, that frequently publish articles on the work and training of the laity:

The Coracle, edited by T. Ralph Morton. The official magazine of the Iona Community. Twice a year. (214 Clyde Street, Glasgow, C. I., Scotland.)

Frontier, of which John Lawrence is the Editor and Mark Gibbs News Editor. The quarterly magazine of the Christian Frontier Council and the Survey Application Trust. (59 Bryanston Street, London, W. 1. American agent: Wm. B. Eerdmans Publishing Company, 255 Jefferson Avenue, Grand Rapids, Mich. 49502.)

Christian Comment, edited by Mark Gibbs for the Audenshaw Foundation. (79 Piccadilly, Manchester 1, England.)

Item, an article service for church magazines edited by Mark

Gibbs for the Audenshaw Foundation. (79 Piccadilly, Manchester 1, England.)

Last (but certainly not least) we would like to mention the various publications of the Department on the Laity of the World Council of Churches. They are not, frankly, always easy to read, but they are quite fundamental to an understanding of the present worldwide interest in the laity. Their periodical, *Laity,* and all their other publications are obtainable through the American Office of the World Council of Churches, 475 Riverside Drive, New York, N.Y. 10027.